lessons with
Clay

lessons with Clay

step-by-step techniques for colorful designs
in hand-thrown and handbuilt tableware

Melisa Dora

SCHIFFER PUBLISHING

4880 Lower Valley Road • Atglen, PA 19310

Other Schiffer Books on Related Subjects:

Ceramics Today, Jeffrey B. Snyder, ISBN 978-0-7643-3465-8

The Ceramics Studio Guide: What Potters Should Know,
Jeff Zamek, ISBN 978-0-7643-5648-3

Library of Congress Control Number: 2022932117

Produced by BlueRed Press Ltd. 2022
Designed by Insight Design Concepts Ltd.
Type set in Montserrat

ISBN: 978-0-7643-6469-3

Printed in India

Published by Schiffer Publishing Ltd.
4880 Lower Valley Read
Atglen, PA 19310
Phone: (610) 593-1777; Fax: (610) 593-2002
Email: Info@schifferbooks.com
Web: www.schifferbooks.com

For our complete selection of fine books on this
and related subjects please visit our website at
www.schifferbooks.com. You may also write for a
free catalog.

Schiffer Publishing's titles are available at special
discounts for bulk purchases for sales promotions
or premiums. Special editions, including
personalized covers, corporate imprints, and
excerpts, can be created in large quantities
for special needs. For more information,
contact the publisher.

We are aways looking for people to
write books on new and related
subjects. If you have an idea for a
book, please contact us at
proposals@schifferbooks.com.

Contents

INTRODUCTION

Lessons with clay offers a contemporary approach to functional ceramics, with illustrated techniques, tips, tools, and projects, both on the wheel and hand building. There are also beautiful, colorful glaze recipes, along with handy tips and guidance on setting up your own studio and how to keep it running sustainably. Understanding the many challenges a pottery studio can present is just as important as making the ceramic work itself.

My name is Melisa Dora, and I'm from southeast London. I am a ceramicist and teacher specializing in hand-thrown tableware. Join me here on an in-depth journey, where I'll share personal and professional experiences developed over ten years of practical work with clay. Being a maker, we tend to show only the finished pieces in our online shop, fair, or gallery, so the consumer never really understands the full cycle. I'm hoping to excite and inspire you by revealing the hidden processes and challenges we go through to create the final pieces throughout this book.

Whether you are a novice, a student, a professional who wishes to review your methods, or even just someone who appreciates the art of handmade things, this book will give you an insight and understanding of how to create beautiful, functional, and decorative objects.

Note that as a ceramicist, patience is a virtue, and perseverance is the key that leads you to creative fulfillment.

My journey

I would like to start off by talking about my journey from being a complete beginner at university to becoming a professional ceramicist and teacher. I was born and raised in England, in southeast London, where I have been working with clay for the past twelve years. My particular passion and focus is directed to hand-thrown, functional, contemporary tableware.

Clay hasn't always been an everyday part of my life. In fact, in my youth, I worked hard and lived for something entirely different. From the ages of five to sixteen, I was a national artistic gymnast competing all over the world. In a way, this important chapter of my life instilled the discipline and determination to lay the foundations for my life with clay.

Sadly, my career as a gymnast ended prematurely due to a severe knee injury during one of my training sessions. This led to a number of ongoing surgeries and physio treatments that, unfortunately, persist to this day. Never would I have thought my life would take such a turn: from enduring endless hours of training with my coach, to wedging pounds of clay, on my own, in my own studio.

I am lucky to have grown up within a creative family environment, and happily this still continues. My mum, who always cooks delicious and beautifully presented meals, sowed the seeds for my tableware admiration. Watching my dad spend long hours in the garage making ingenious little inventions with whatever was on hand was inspiring. Even my sister transforming any boring school book into a masterpiece with her imaginative drawings fed me artistically.

I thrived at school during my art and design lessons since they allowed me to fully express myself. The exposure to this hive of creativity has significantly influenced my career with clay.

My first encounter with clay

In 2005 I began an Art and Design Foundation course at Camberwell College of Art in London, which in turn led me to studying Materials Practice at Brighton University in 2006. Here I was able to experiment and gain practical knowledge in wood, metal, plastics, and ceramics. This is where my exploration of ceramics really developed in earnest. My specialized material choices in my second year were ceramics and wood. I further developed my skills for one more year, with the addition of an MDes (master of design) level, where I had the wonderful opportunity to attend studio-based placements, finally graduating in 2010 with a first-class honors degree.

During a throwing demonstration at university, my tutor, the ceramicist Louisa Taylor, made it look so simple. However, when I tried, my clay flew off the wheel and water splattered everywhere. I soon realized it was a highly skilled practice. It took me a while to master the wheel, but It made me think differently. I had struggled with the academic side of university due to my dyslexia, but the wheel made me focus my thoughts. It quickly became apparent that the only thing that made me stop thinking about everything else and concentrate fully was that spinning piece of clay in front of me.

Upon completion of my university years, I didn't feel quite ready to set up my own studio. The plan of action was to work as a studio assistant with various artists to gain more experience. Louisa Taylor took me on as her assistant at Cockpit Arts, Deptford, in London. By the end of my time there, I had worked with almost every maker on the second floor, which ranged across various skills, such as placing tiny transfers onto ceramic jewelry with Allison Wiffen and silkscreen printing onto clothing for my dearest friends Emma and Rachael Nissim.

I loved the artistic community at Cockpit Arts. Working under experienced professionals and makers filled me with an immense desire to put to practice everything that I had learned. This gave me the courage to set up my own studio.

Finding a studio

My first so-called studio was in my parents' garage. My dad provided me with a small space wedged between his classic Mini Cooper and his numerous bottles of homemade wine. With the help of my family and friends, I bought a wheel, assembled a couple of shelves, and off I went.

That garage turned out to be one of the coldest places on earth (or at least that's how it felt at the time), which really affected my work flow. Luckily, a friend's recommendation led me to a local shared ceramic studio run by Roland Austin, an amazingly experienced and humble potter from whom I learned an invaluable amount.

Roland was truly inspiring. He had a calm and gentle manner of dealing with all aspects of running a pottery studio and handed on the kind of wisdom you don't usually come across. Sadly, Roland passed away in 2020. I am eternally grateful for the opportunity to have had such an amazing mentor.

Running my own pottery business was not easy at the beginning, meaning that for many years I worked very long hours in various part-time and occasionally full-time jobs to help fund my studio and rent. This hard work eventually paid off, since I finally got the keys to my own space in 2016. This is where my business started to unfold. A wide net of possibilities expanded right before my eyes—it felt like all my boundaries had disappeared and creativity was within my reach, far more than ever before.

The purpose of my works

It used to be easy to spot the reflection of my heritage and family background (my dad is Turkish and my mum Swiss) on all of my earliest pieces. Turkish architecture, patterns, and colors commonly found on Iznik tiles were at the forefront of everything I made, along with the precision and attention to detail found in Switzerland.

After spending hours painting intricate patterns onto my work, carving out details, and making a vast amount of porcelain jewelry, I started to reinvent my style to focus more on my passion for color in glazes, along with more symmetrical contemporary shapes. I found it a challenge to change direction, since it felt like a complete reinvention of what made me comfortable, but it was a change for the better.

Left: In 2018 I expanded my studio so I had the opportunity to teach more students. This is where I currently work.

Teaching

Having my own studio also meant I could give something back to the community through teaching a variety of classes. It has helped bring friends, families, and like-minded people together, allowing a short amount of time to destress and to express themselves creatively. In turn, sharing various lessons over the years and reviewing methods helped me appreciate my own professional development. The love, joy, and fulfillment that comes with meeting new students—every smile and giggle, and the surprised look in their eyes—fills me with so much motivation.

Clay can bring you success, surprises, failures, passion, and discipline all in one go. I hope my in-depth journey with ceramics throughout this book will fill you with true knowledge and the desire to pick up some clay and create to your heart's content. Inspiration can be found anywhere—it's all around us.

Right: With the improved studio, new ideas quickly surfaced. Suddenly my work style drastically changed. My new variety of colors and forms attracted much more attention, of the kind I had never had before. Soon I began to work on a number of tableware collections and freelance commissions for much-larger markets. Since then, most of my pieces are destined to be used for gastronomy, home décor, and floristry.

CLAY SELECTION AND PREPARATION

CLAY SELECTION AND PREPARATION

CLAY SELECTION

Sourcing the ideal clay for the type of work you want to produce is a good starting point. However, deciding which one works for you is a trial-and-error process. Clay can be bought from many pottery suppliers in a wide range of colors, textures, and weights. It can even be dug from the ground, but that requires research and testing.

There are a few questions you will need to ask yourself before deciding on the right clay to use:

Are you hand-building or hand-throwing?

A smooth elastic clay is best for throwing, and a grogged clay is more stable for hand-building. Grog is a type of clay that has already been fired and then ground up to various degrees of fineness. Used in proportion with ordinary clay, it reduces shrinkage and makes cracking less likely.

To what temperature are you firing your clay?

There are two main types of firing: earthenware and stoneware. Earthenware clay is fired to a lower temperature than stoneware, 1,922°F–2,102°F (1,050°C–1,150°C), making it more porous and less durable. Stoneware temperatures range

between 2,192°F and 2,372°F (1,200°C–1,300°C). Since my work is functional and made for everyday use, I choose to work with a white stoneware clay and glazes that fire up to cone 7 (2,264°F/ 1,240°C) in my electric kiln.

What effect would you like to achieve once fired?

To discover which clay works best for you, simply purchase a variety of 2.2 lb. (1 kg) sample-clay bags from a pottery supplier and test them against each other before committing to a large order. Find out which one feels the most comfortable and best matches the overall result you are aiming to achieve.

It is not necessary to glaze a pot in order to obtain interesting effects and colors. This can occur naturally within the clay, and each raw material will present a unique result of its own. However, should your piece be destined for eating or drinking, a crucial aspect for tableware is making sure you are using a food-safe glaze within the interior surface.

My goal has been to find a clay with a smooth firing surface that will hold my colorful glazes well. This is mainly driven from a functional perspective, since food and drink will be served from my work. I want the overall feeling of drinking or eating off my work to be a comfortable and enjoyable experience.

I have always been fascinated with how different clay bodies change color from beginning—out of the clay bag—to end (after the last firing). You'll notice that the color starts changing during the drying stages and alters more dramatically after each kiln firing.

No.	Clay
1	Porcelain
2	50% grogged gray mixed with 50% white stoneware
3	50% Vulcan black (smooth) mixed with 50% white stoneware
4	50% Vulcan black (coarse) mixed with 50% white stoneware
5	Grogged gray
6	50% grogged pink mixed with 50% white stoneware
7	Earthstone smooth-textured crank
8	White stoneware
9	Fleck stoneware
10	Lavafleck
11	Vulcan black (smooth)
12	Vulcan black (coarse)

MIXING CLAYS

This can open up a range of textures and colors, but you must ensure the different clays have a similar shrinkage rate and firing temperature; otherwise your pot may fail in the kiln firing due to the different tensions within each clay body.

Throwing with grogged clay can feel uncomfortable on your hands, depending on the size of grog—plus it adds the challenge of trimming your piece smoothly. This can be resolved by the addition of a smoother clay, which will make it more comfortable to work with. In turn this can alter the color during firing, but you can produce really interesting effects by combining clays together. To fully understand how to mix clays and ensure they are fully homogenized, see the next stages in clay preparation on the following pages.

Below: Twelve different stoneware clay test tiles demonstrating three stages without any glaze. The top row is clay in its raw state, fresh out of the bag. The middle is after its first bisque firing (1,000°C/1,832°F) and the bottom row is after its second firing to cone 7 (1,240°C/2,264°F). In some of the examples I have mixed two clays together.

Below: A variety of experiments using smooth and grogged throwing clays fired to cone 7. I used a 50/50 ratio when mixing these clays together and glazed each cylinder in a glossy transparent glaze (recipe on page 117). You can also experiment with a range of percentages for each clay when mixing them together—it's fun and makes the clay feel more personal to you.

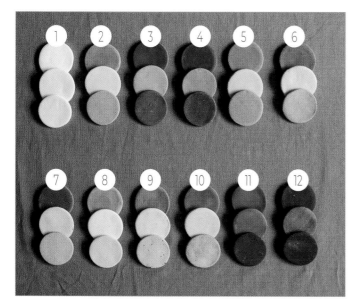

Shrinkage

Every clay you will work with will have a unique shrinkage rate, which will affect the measurements of your finished piece. This is normally displayed within the description when purchasing, or you could test this yourself by making test tiles or even a clay ruler. If you have particular measurements you want to produce, whether it's on the wheel or hand-building, you need to calculate for this percentage before making. Clay will start shrinking from its drying stages and also when fired in a kiln. This is due to water evaporating from within the clay and then burning off organic matter throughout the first firing and vitrification in the second firing.

Below: Example of how much one of my hand-thrown tumblers has shrunk from freshly thrown to glaze fired.

Clay Preparation

This is the first stage in making any piece, whether on the wheel or hand-building. Without this process, you are likely to obtain air pockets in the making stages, which can cause problems further down the line.

The two clay-wedging methods I use most in my studio are "Ram's Head" and "Cut, Slam, Repeat."

The table and surface you are preparing the clay on must be strong and able to absorb the moisture within the clay. The height of the table is also an important aspect. It should be in-line with your hip, meaning your back is straight, not hunched. A surface that will absorb the clay's moisture is ideal; look for wooden worktops without a glossy finish, cotton canvas material, or even a plaster bat.

Ram's Head

Start by getting a good amount of clay to wedge, with the intention to divide it into your desired weight to throw or hand-build with.

1. Hold the clay on your workbench and place your thumbs on the top and your palms on the sides.

2. Push the clay down and away from your body. The clay will naturally roll back. Make sure your fingers are supporting the sides and squeezing in slightly as you roll the clay back. Do not press too firmly; otherwise you will flatten the clay.

3. Roll the clay in toward you. Try not to fold it in too much, since you will trap air in-between the clay. Short and quick movements are best. You want the air to escape and not to create any air pockets. Repeat steps 2 and 3 around twenty to thirty times with clay fresh out of the bag, but double this number if it is reclaimed clay.

4. After a few movements a ram's head with spiral ears will begin to form.

If your piece is forming into a long rectangle, pat the sides in, but always hold the sides as you continue to wedge.

When you have finished wedging, wire your piece in half to see if there are any air pockets. If there are, then you will need to keep working on it.

1

2

3

4

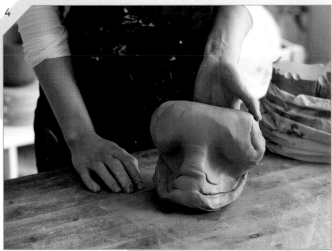

Air pockets—go back and rework the clay.

No air pockets—perfect!

Cut, Slam, and Repeat technique

This method is perfect if you have a variety of clay consistencies that you want to blend together. It is also a great method for combining two different clay bodies together, as shown in the experiments on page 15.

1. Prepare a rectangular-shaped lump of clay and place it at a slight angle toward you. Place a potter's wire through the clay from the table to the ceiling.

2. Grab the piece of clay from the top that you have just wired, flip it, and slam it on top of the other facing you.

3. Grab the two pieces that have been slammed together. Flip and slam it down again so the top piece is now at the bottom.
   Roll your piece of clay to the left and slam it down in the shape you started with (step 1), ready to cut, slam, and repeat again.

If you notice air pockets when you cut the clay in half, keep working and wedging until there are no air pockets and the clay is sufficiently mixed. If there are still air pockets, examine your technique—you may be slamming the clay down in a way that causes air to be trapped inside the two pieces of clay.

WEIGHING

4. Every product has a particular weight to it. I weigh each ball of clay out before working with it on the wheel. This is so I can get consistency within the range of products I make. Finding balance in your pieces is important. Not too heavy and thick, or too thin and fragile. Experimenting with a range of weights is a great way to find out what works for you.

5. After weighing the clay and cutting off a piece, wedge it a few more times and then pat the clay into a ball, ready to throw on the wheel or into the shape you need for hand-building. (5a and 5b)

Reclaim buckets.

A SUSTAINABLE STUDIO

Pottery studios are becoming increasingly popular around the world. So it's important to develop and abide by sustainable habits and methods within your own studio. A little help with the environment can go a long way.

Reclaim

Having a reclaim setup in your studio will prolong the life of the clay you are using. I reclaim, reuse, and recycle every little bit, including the water I throw with on the wheel. There are many ways to reclaim clay, but I like to keep each stage of reclaim in separate buckets. This setup keeps my studio organized. However, make sure you keep buckets separate if you are working with more than one clay.

The buckets

1. **Clay to dry:** Before—or even after—you trim your pieces, you may decide that you don't want to keep them because the base is too thin, it has wobbly areas, or it has uneven walls that may not have been spotted at the making stages. All of these pieces are put into this bucket to dry out, so you can reuse the clay. They need to dry out

1

completely before adding any water or slurry to them, so leave the lid open to dry them out. Please be careful of dust if you are leaving the lid open to dry these pieces.

Occasionally, I put such pieces in a tray under my kiln when it is cooling down from a firing, so they can dry out quicker. You cannot rework fired clay, so this stage is really important. If you're unsure whether your pot will survive firing or you are unhappy with it, it's best to reclaim this clay so you can rework it for another piece.

2. **Slurry:** Pour all of your throwing water, clay mishaps, accidents, and slurry that's left in your wheel pan at the end of your throwing session into this bucket.

3. **Trimmings:** Trimmings/turnings are placed into this bucket.

It's a good idea to label your buckets so that in the heat of the moment you don't throw the waste into the wrong container. If space is restricted, you can use one bucket to reclaim your clay scraps, trimmings and slurry. Just make sure that if you have leather-hard pieces, they will need to dry out completely (bone dry) before placing them in this bucket, since they will not break down easily, which will make it harder for you to rework into new clay.

2

3

The process

As the trimmings and dried-clay bucket start to fill up, pour your slurry bucket into these two buckets—but make sure the clay is completely dry before this step.

Mixing your throwing water/slurry with your reclaim will make the clay stronger, and it means you won't have to use any extra water for this. You do not need to wait for trimmings to dry completely before adding the slurry, since they are thin and will break down easily. Leave these buckets to settle overnight so all the clay particles have time to break down into a slushy usable liquid.

The drying stages

A plaster bat is an extremely useful piece of equipment to have in a pottery studio. It can vary in size depending on your workload and is used mainly to dry out your reclaimed clay, rework, and use again. You can also use them for clay preparation, as shown on page 16. I have a few plaster bats in my studio, which I use regularly. They can be easily made or you can buy them from pottery suppliers. You will need a mold to pour the plaster into, or you can make it yourself with wooden boards and clamps. Different plasters will have a variety of measuring instructions to mix with water. Please read the instructions carefully and wear a respiratory mask at all times when working with plaster.

Plaster is the best way to dry your clay, since it sucks out moisture and enables you to rework the clay into a state where you can throw or hand build again.

If you are making your own, the thickness should be approximately 1.9 in. (5 cm) so there is a good amount of depth for moisture to be collected within the clay. If a plaster bat is too thin, it will be prone to breaking easily with the weight of clay on top, or it will absorb the water within the clay too fast and stay wet. Try propping your plaster board above the surface it is sitting on to allow constant air flow to travel underneath; this allows the clay and plaster bat to dry out evenly. I use kiln props for this.

The shape is dependent on your preference, but rectangular ones seem to work very well and are space saving. If looked after, they can last a very long time. Make sure you chamfer all sides and edges of your plaster bat; any sharp edges can chip easily and contaminate the clay. Furthermore, this contamination could cause the plaster to explode in the kiln while firing.

1. Transfer the reclaimed clay (from the bucket you left overnight) onto a plaster board.

2. Smooth out the clay onto the plaster board, making sure there are no peaks within the clay, since these parts can dry out quicker. The clay needs to dry evenly throughout. (2a)

The length of the next stage all depends on the temperature in your studio and the amount of clay you are reclaiming. In winter months I can leave clay to dry out on my plaster board for up to two or three days. During the summer months it can be ready the next day. (2b)

3. Keep checking the clay consistency. If you can lift up the edges of your clay from the plaster, this will mean it is ready. Flip over the clay surface that's been in contact with the plaster. You will need to keep checking this, since you don't want the clay to get too hard; otherwise you cannot rework it. In warmer climates, you may not even need to flip the clay.

4. Gently press the clay down into the plaster to make a level surface.

When you are happy with the clay's consistency from the plaster board, you will need to rework and wedge the reclaimed clay, as shown on pages 16–19. Make sure you spend more time wedging reclaimed clay than you do normally, since this clay has a variety of components mixed together—such as slurry, trimmings, and bone-dry clay—so all the particles need to be wedged properly in order for it to be a new, healthy clay mix to work with again.

5. You may have clay to reclaim that will not hold its shape on a plaster board. This can be fixed by using a plaster mold with walls.

This has been made by using a cooking tin turned upside down and placed inside a large plastic box, with a space of 1.5 inches or more all around and above the tin. Secure the tin down using clay coils. Pour plaster into this box and wait for it to dry completely. Plastic containers are best for this process, since the plaster will easily pop out. You may need to coat the inside walls of your container with plaster soap for a smoother release of the plaster when it's solid.

CLAY TRAP

A clay trap will prolong the life of your sinks, pipes, and drainage system in your studio. You should not pour your throwing water, clay, or glaze materials directly down the sink, since it will block your pipes and cause (expensive) problems further down the line. It will also harm the environment and contribute to a unsustainable practice.

Clay traps can be bought from a variety of suppliers, or you can easily make one yourself. It sits under your sink and keeps clay particles from going directly down your drain. You can eventually rework these particles into usable clay.

Try to avoid pouring unwanted glaze into your clay trap. Glaze tools can be washed up in a separate bucket. Leave components to settle overnight and siphon off the water the next day. I have a mystery glaze bucket in my studio where I put any unwanted glaze tests. I then go through the mixing and sieving process, as shown on pages 122–23, and use it on my work. I use it only on the outside of pieces, due to there being many components within the glaze that may not be food safe.

When you notice your clay trap filling up, you need to clean it out by drying the clay waste and either reworking it into new clay or disposing it if you have mixed glaze into it. This can be done in many ways. I have two large bisque-fired bowls that I put my clay trap waste into. The bisque bowls absorb the moisture and aid the drying process.

If you do not have a clay trap, place a bucket inside your sink and wash tools and equipment in there. Let the clay sink to the bottom of the bucket, and the following day you can siphon off the water.

RECYCLING AND OTHER ASPECTS

Packaging materials

There are many other steps you can take to ensure you are helping the environment around you by using recyclable, compostable, and biodegradable packaging materials. If you are selling your work online, it can be very difficult and time-consuming to package safely and securely. I try to use as many recycled materials as possible when sending orders around the world—such as biodegradable packing peanuts, recyclable packing tape, and corrugated cardboard to wrap my work. If you have space, keep unwanted cardboard boxes, since they always come in handy.

Reuse

If you have any fired pottery that you are unable to use or sell because of faults, then try to reuse these pieces and not throw them away. They can be sold as seconds, broken to pieces as crocks for plant pots, or even turned into beautiful mosaics.

Energy consumption

Your electricity supplier could also have a large impact on your energy consumption. Try looking into a green energy supplier; they are becoming more popular and widely available for a variety of businesses and households.

Try to avoid half-load firings where you are not using the kiln efficiently. Please see page 145 on how to pack your kiln when firing.

Little steps can really go a long way. Not everything has to be done at once; take your time to research ways to help the environment within your studio and to reduce waste.

HAND-BUILDING

HAND-BUILDING

Hand-building is one of many pottery techniques which doesn't use the pottery wheel as its sole equipment/purpose. It is also a much more accessible method of making ceramics without needing any large equipment.

I am going to demonstrate how to make a beautiful breakfast set by using two hand-building techniques. These techniques can be further explored into a vast number of shapes and sizes once you feel confident.

All the pieces in this chapter have been made using stoneware, smooth-textured, grogged clay. They have been bisque-fired to 1,832°F/1,000°C and glaze-fired to cone 7: 2,264°F/1,240°C.

Hand-building is best made with clay that has grit/grog in it so it can be built up. A clay body that is too smooth and elastic can collapse easily. If you don't have a kiln, you can also practice hand-building with air-dry clay. However, air-dry clay is used mainly for decorative pieces, not functional ones.

TOOLS

The most useful piece of equipment that you may not have at home is a turntable / banding wheel. The wheel helps you work freely on all sides of your piece; it saves constantly lifting and turning, which can distort the clay. Other useful tools:

1. Canvas material
2. Cookie cutters
3. Old credit card
4. Paint brush
5. Potter's knife
6. Potter's needle/pin
7. Rolling pin
8. Rubber kidneys—different strengths (green: medium flexibility; red: soft)
9. Ruler
10. Sponge
11. Sponge on a stick
12. Turntable / banding wheel
13. Wooden guide sticks
14. Wooden mark-making and finishing tools
15. Wooden spatula
16. Metal serrated kidney

Left: Hand-built breakfast set

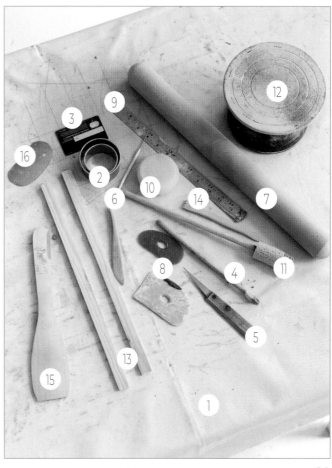

PINCHING

The pinching technique is a great way to start hand-building and provides you with the foundation on how to work and manipulate clay into a variety of forms. You will find that parts of this technique are used throughout this chapter. For anyone who has never worked with clay before, I really recommend starting with this technique. You can get a real sense of clay's likes and dislikes and how it works in your hands. In other techniques you may not be able to notice straightaway what has gone wrong or how to fix an issue, but with pinching there are a variety of small hand movements you can make in order to produce a vessel you feel proud of.

BOWL

Depending on size, this is a great bowl for jam, honey, salt, pepper, sugar, fruit, yogurt, and cereal.

Making measurements:

Small pinched bowl for condiments

Clay (all dependent on the function): 1.7–5 oz. (50–150 g)

Dimensions: 2.4–3 in. diameter x 1.2–1.9 in. height (6–8 cm x 3–5 cm)

Medium pinched bowl for fruit, yogurt, or cereal

Clay: 14–17.6 oz. (400–500 g)

Dimensions: 4.7–5.9 in. diameter x 1.5–2.4 in. height (12–15 cm x 4–6 cm)

Prepare your clay as shown on pages 16–19 and weigh into your desired weight.

1. Pat the clay into a round ball. The rounder it is, the easier it will be to make the pinch pot.

2. Hold the ball of clay in one hand and, with the other, press your thumb into the middle of the ball up to your knuckle.

3. Gently pinch with your thumb and fingers down and around the pot.

   The aim is to try to get the same wall thickness all the way around your pot, no matter what shape you end up with. The base should be approximately 0.2–0.4 in. (0.5–1 cm) in thickness. I tend to swap hands throughout the pinching process.

4. To make a curved interior and exterior shape, gently squeeze the walls outward from the base to the rim while holding the pinched pot in the palm of one hand. It's better to start off with having the walls thick so you can work with them, rather than having them too thin, since it may flop and collapse.

5. Place your pot on a nonstick surface—such as a cotton canvas material or wooden board—and press or tap the base down so you have a flat and leveled surface. (5a)

   You do not need to do this if you want a curved base, but since this pot is being used for serving food, the base needs to be flat, so nothing spills. (5b)

6. If you can see any cracks starting to appear in the clay, apply a small amount of water with a sponge to rework that area, then smooth it over with your fingertips.

   After making the main shape, you can use a wooden spatula or a rubber kidney to pat down areas and smooth out the exterior walls. A nice effect is to leave some of your fingerprint marks within the clay.

TIP

I particularly like the uneven surface on the rim with pinch pots, since it's the complete opposite to my usual thrown work, which has clean uniform rims. If you want straight, level rims, then you can turn your pinch pot upside down and pat the rim on a flat surface, or you can use a potters' knife to slice away a thin layer on the top.

---

7. Finished bowls.

   Start to experiment with more clay and test a variety of shapes and sizes. When using more clay, be aware of the stability around the base and walls.

8. If you want to give height to your pinch bowl, you could add clay coils. Just make sure you smooth out the interior and exterior joints of these coils as you build the walls up.

Bud Vase

This is another great way to really understand how clay works and its boundaries—the possibilities are endless with this technique. The aim of this process is to make two pinch pots that are the same size, and join them together to make a hollow sphere that you can then shape into a variety of forms.

This demonstration shows how to make a small bud vase to accompany a table setting.

Making measurements:
Clay: 5 oz. (150 g) for each pinch pot
Dimensions: 2.9 in. diameter x 1.6 in. height (7.5 x 4 cm) for each pinch pot

Prepare your clay as shown on pages 16–19 and weigh two 5 oz. (150 g) pieces of clay.

1. Repeat steps 1–4 on page 32 with both balls of clay. Most importantly, you want to end up with two pinch pots that have the same circumference at the top.

   Try not to make the rims too thin, because you will need excess clay to work with when closing and shaping the form.

2. Make sure the rims are level so it will be easier for you to attach them together. If they are uneven, you can always cut them back with a knife to make them level, or pat them gently on a flat surface.

3. Cross-hatch both rims of the pinch pots with a serrated metal kidney or a potter's knife.

4. Apply some water to both pinch pots with a paint brush and wait till the clay gets sticky.

5. Connect both rims of the two pinch pots—the water will naturally ooze out. It's really important to get a strong bond here because you won't be reinforcing the inside joint; you can make the joint stronger only from the exterior wall for this particular project.

6. Holding the closed form in one hand, use your fingertips on your other hand to bring clay from one pinch pot down to the other to reinforce the joint. Go all the way around, making sure it is fully joined. You could also use a wooden rib for this step.

1

4

2

5

3

6

7. At this stage, your piece will look like a hollow sphere, which you can now shape. Patting and shaping your hollowed form may take a few tries to really get a sense of how your clay works. Some clays react differently from others.

   You will soon realize that if you have made your two pinch pots too thin, then they could collapse or crack in places while shaping.

8. Using a wooden spatula or a wooden stick, shape your hollowed form. (8a)

   I have transformed mine into an egg shape. (8b)

9. Place the form on a flat surface and pat it down to create a flat base for it to stand.

   If your clay is still really soft, use a heat gun or a hairdryer on a low setting to dry out the clay slightly. Or you can leave it to dry naturally before moving onto the next step.

10. Define your shape further with a wooden spatula on all sides, including the base, making sure it will sit level on a flat surface.

11. Using a potter's knife or a circular cutting tool, cut a hole where you would like the opening for the flower to sit.

12

13a

13b

14

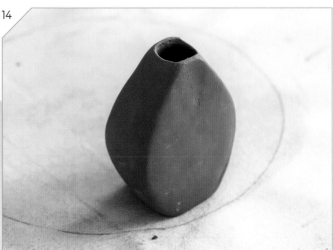

12. Pinch and extend the neck of the vase to define the shape further. After making a hole and shaping it, your piece may become less resistant and lose its shape slightly, since the air will now be able to escape. If this happens, wait for your piece to dry further so it can gain more stability.

13. Finishing touches: accentuate the form by finishing it off with a bit more patting, and smooth out the surface by using a wooden spatula, soft rubber kidney, or the back of a spoon. (13a)

    You can also add textures at this stage with a variety of tools and materials. (13b)

14. Finished vase

TIP

If you would like to experiment further with this technique and make a variety of hollowed forms, always make sure there is a hole in place for air to escape during kiln firing. Without a hole, you could run the risk of it exploding in the kiln due to trapped air.

SLAB BUILDING

This technique demonstrates how a rolled-out sheet of clay
can be turned into a beautiful side plate for breakfast, lunch, or
dinner, plus a tumbler to use for cold or hot drinks.

SIDE PLATE

Making measurements:

Clay: 28 oz. (800 g)

Dimensions: 8.6 in. diameter x 0.4 in. height (22 x 1 cm)

Prepare your clay as shown on pages 16–19 and weigh out 28 oz. (800 g) of clay. You will need a sheet of material/canvas to roll your clay onto and wooden guides measuring 0.2 in. (0.5 cm) in thickness. The material you are using should be able to absorb the clay's moisture so you can lift the clay away easily. Make sure the surface you are rolling clay onto is completely flat.

1. Place your clay in the middle of the sticks and flatten it down slightly by applying a small amount of pressure with your hands or a rolling pin.

2. Use a wooden rolling pin to roll out the clay. Start from the middle, then roll toward you. Go back to the middle and roll away from you. This will help release any air pockets within the clay.

   Every so often, lift the slab of clay from the material, flip over, and turn it around to allow air to flow underneath. Repeat step 2 after this. It will be a lot easier to roll the clay out after you have done this.

3. Once your clay is level and in line with the measuring sticks, pop any air bubbles within the clay. (3a)

   Smooth over with a kidney / wooden rib. This further combines particles within the clay and gets rid of any textures you may have picked up / don't want from the material you are using. Leaving any air pockets within the clay may ruin the overall look and finish of your piece. (3b)

4. I made a cardboard template measuring 8.6in. (22cm) to cut out the circle for my plate.

   Remove the excess clay you are not using and place it back into your clay bag ready to use for another project.

   The next few steps are best achieved on a turntable/ banding wheel.

5. Place the clay circle carefully on a flat wooden board so you can position it on a turntable. Try not to bend the clay too much when transporting it. Clay has memory, so if you distort it too much at this stage, it will remember it during the firing stages.

6a

6b

7

8

9a

9b

6. Using your thumb and forefinger, carefully lift up and pinch the sides of the circle to create the edges of your plate. (6a)

   Start with a small amount of pressure and then keep rotating the plate to work on the exterior walls. (6b)

7. Pinch the rims with your thumb and forefinger to make a smoother, softer rim. Having a sharp rim on any tableware piece is prone to chipping.

8. The next three steps are all similar, but you will be using different tools. First, press your thumb on your dominant hand into your other hand's palm, with the walls of the plate in between. This creates a curved inside edge to the plate.

9. Repeat step 8, but with a sponge and the curved edge of a rubber kidney. (9a–b)

   Let your plate dry really slowly on a flat surface and try not to move it around too much. I usually place a wooden board on top, since this stops the edges of the plate lifting up while drying.

10. Detailed close-up of the edge.

11. The finished plate

TUMBLER

Making measurements:

Clay: 17.6 oz. (500 g) for main vessel and base

Dimensions: Using a 10 oz. coffee cup: 4.5 in. height x 3.5 in. top diameter (11.5 x 9 cm)

The card template I'm using for this technique is made from a used 10 oz. coffee cup, which I cut and rolled out flat. I added an extra 0.4 in. (1 cm) to each end of my own cardboard template, so a beveled edge can be cut when joining the two ends together. Once fired, this coffee cup will have an 8 oz. volume. This technique can be used with a variety of cup sizes; it is entirely up to you which size you choose to make your tumbler.

Prepare your clay as shown on pages 16–19 and weigh out 17.6 oz. (500 g) to be used for the main vessel and base.

1. Repeat Steps 1–3 in plate making on pages 44–45. Once your clay is level and in line with the measuring guides, place your tumbler template on the clay and cut around it.

2. Remove any unwanted clay and wedge to use for the next step.

3. With the excess clay from step 2, roll out a separate bit of clay for the base of the tumbler, using the same measuring guides as before. Cut out a circle, using a cookie cutter, measuring approximately 2.4 in. (6 cm) in diameter. Place the base to one side.

4. On the right-hand end of the clay tumbler template, place a straight edge tool 0.4 in. (1 cm) in from the edge and hold your knife at a 45-degree angle. Cut a beveled edge on this line.

    Flip the template over to the right, so the beveled edge you just made is facing the surface you are working on and is now on the left-hand side.

5. Repeat step 4. The two ends—the edge facing you on the right, and the edge facing the surface you are working on on the left—of the tumbler should now be at an angle cut to approximately 45 degrees.

    Pick your tumbler template up. If the clay feels really floppy, let it dry naturally or use a heat gun / hairdryer so the clay will hold its structure better for the next step. Don't apply too much heat, since the clay will crack when shaping and it will be difficult to join the two ends together.

6. Form the tumbler template into a cylinder by connecting the two beveled ends together. Make sure they align well, then overlap them slightly so they can be smoothed out in the next step.

7. Smooth out the joint by gently placing your fingers inside the tumbler so you can rest it against the interior wall. Using your other hand, press against the joint and smooth out in the same direction as the joint. This is where grog clay comes in handy, since it keeps its shape. (You will work on the interior joint in step 16.)

8. As the tumbler dries, continue to form it more into a cylinder by placing it on a wooden board and shaping the interior and exterior with both hands. Using a banding wheel will help.

9. Cross-hatch the edges of the bottom of the tumbler and the base.

10. Apply water on the base template and the tumbler where you have just marked.

11. Secure the tumbler on top of the base template. Pick up the tumbler and gently pat it down on a flat surface so the base joins to the tumbler well.

12. Cut the excess clay away from the base where you have just made the joint.

13

16

14

17a

15

17b

13. Smooth the exterior joint, using a sponge and a rubber kidney. At the same time, keep one hand inside to support the structure.

14. Turn the tumbler upside down and use a wooden spatula to gently pat and shape the exterior walls and base.

15. Use a rubber kidney to soften the edges and add a beveled edge to the base.

16. Finishing touches: Use a curved edge tool and a sponge on a stick to blend and neaten the interior joint. You can also do the same for the inside joint that connects to the base.

17. Since this is a cup to drink from, the rim should be rounded and not too sharp. Pinch the rim with your thumb and forefinger. (17a)

   Soften it out, using a sponge. (17b)

18. Finished Tumbler

19. Finished, unglazed pieces of the breakfast set.

THROWING

THROWING

Throwing is my favorite technique in pottery, although it wasn't an instant attraction for me. It can be difficult to master at first, but when you start to develop a rhythm with your hands, you will begin to love it. Patience, practice, and repetition are fundamental.

Throwing doesn't have to be associated with functional ware; there are endless possibilities you can explore on the wheel, such as sculptural and decorative work too.

Every guidebook and video will have different techniques and instructions on how to make certain objects, which can make it all very confusing to begin with, but there are always a few fundamental steps you need to start you off. My instructions are here as a guide, but you may find that you will naturally end up with certain hand movements of your own.

Five important points to remember throughout the making stages on the pottery wheel:

1. The interior of your pot is just as important as the exterior. This is often forgotten.

2. Depending on whether you are right- or left-handed, your hands should always be positioned on the wheel between three and six o'clock for right handers and six and nine o'clock for left handers.

3. Always spin the wheel first, then place your hands or tools onto the clay.

4. Release your hands slowly when finishing a step or stopping the wheel. Releasing too quickly can make your pot veer off-center.

5. Make sure you coat the clay and your hands with water. If there is not enough water, then the clay will get sticky and it could potentially go off-center.

I have demonstrated two simple shapes in this chapter, since I feel it's really important to gain confidence and perfect these forms before moving on to more-complex ideas.

THE POTTER'S WHEEL

Pottery wheels can last a lifetime if looked after, and there are a variety of wheels to choose from to suit every need. We all differ, so purchase what feels right and comfortable for you, not anyone else. Unless you are planning to teach!

Positioning

It is very important to ensure that you have the correct height for your wheel and the chair or stool you sit on. You shouldn't feel any strain or discomfort. If you do, adjust the height of your stool or that of your wheel. Make sure you take regular breaks and stretches. The wheel can be addictive and time passes very quickly, so small physical breaks are necessary.

Note that if you ever feel strain on your hands or back while working on the wheel, this could be due to your clay not being soft enough. If this is the case, place this clay to one side, poke holes in it, then fill with water, close the holes, and wrap it up in a plastic sheet or back in the clay bag. Leave this clay to absorb the water, and use a clay that is easier and softer to work with.

I am right-handed, so all of my instructions in this chapter use my right foot on the peddle and the wheel spinning counterclockwise. There are wheels you can purchase with a function to spin the wheel clockwise if you are left-handed.

The peddle should be in line with your right leg and shouldn't be too far out. Your leg should be bent while pressing down on the peddle, and it should feel comfortable and not strenuous.

TOOLS

There are many tools you can make yourself—from old credit cards to wooden throwing ribs. I use the following tools when throwing:

1. Medium-strength rubber kidney (green)
2. Pointed wooden tool
3. Potter's needle
4. Potter's knife
5. Small sponge
6. Soft strength rubber kidney (red)
7. Sponge on a stick
8. Potter's wire

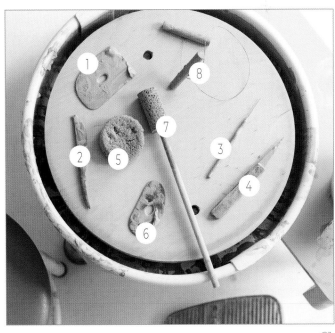

Making a cylinder

This is the most important shape to learn first on the wheel. From this shape, you can begin to make a variety of other forms. The best way to learn is repetition.

About 14 oz. (400 g) of clay is a good starting weight when learning to throw. Wedge a good amount of clay, using either of the techniques explained on pages 16–19, and divide into 14 oz. balls.

Coning and centering

This is the first step in getting your clay secure and uniform to the wheel. It is also another method in preparing your clay, similar to the wedging technique. Coning is forcing the clay toward the center, using both hands to bring the clay up to a point. It helps reduce air pockets and aligns the particles, which will homogenize the clay.

Wheel speed: for steps 1–9, fastest

First, get comfortable and make sure your tools and a jug of water are nearby. Check that the height of your chair and wheel are appropriate. The pedal should be in line with your leg and not too far out. Since my studio can get really cold at times, I make sure I throw with warm water. This really helps loosen joints in the hands, making the movements you make on the wheel more fluid.

1. Place the ball of prepared clay into the center of the wheel head and pat it down gently on all sides so it is secure. Tug it slightly so you are confident that it is firmly on the wheel and it's not going to fly off when you press the peddle. Try not to flatten it too much, since it will be difficult to cone in and center.

2. Press your foot right down on the peddle to its fastest speed and wet your hands and the clay. Wrap both hands around the ball of clay and press down slightly with your thumbs while the wheel is spinning. This is further securing the clay to the wheel head.

3. Keep the wheel spinning at its fastest speed and make sure your elbows are resting firmly on your thighs throughout the coning process. Push the clay with your left palm toward the center in a diagonal line. At the same time, use the fingers on your right hand to squeeze and push the clay in toward your left palm. This will automatically bring the clay up to a cone shape. (3a)

   Try not to squeeze too much from the base, as the clay may come away from the wheel. (3b)

   Gradually bring your hands up with the clay to create a cone. (3c)

4. Release your right hand and continue to hold this shape with your left hand while the wheel is spinning—remembering to keep adding water to the clay. Press down on the top of the cone either with your right fist or by using your thumbs. The outside walls of your centered clay should be aligned.

   With 14 oz. of clay, I usually cone up and press down two or three times before making the base.

5. As you are pressing down, try pushing the clay down at an angle on the exterior wall and squeeze in slightly with your left hand.

6. If you press down from the top only, you may end up with a mushroom shape. If this happens, squeeze the sides in and round off the edges down to the wheel head with your fingertips.

Throughout my years of teaching, I have noticed that using more pressure with your right hand pulling toward your left palm when coning up will get your clay centered. You will also have more control if your hands are wrapped around the clay when coning, as opposed to being straight. It's all about knowing how much pressure to use in these first stages.

Always ease into throwing slowly rather than at full force. If you feel your elbows moving away from your thighs, place them back down, since this will provide more control. You do not want to see any movement back and forth with your elbows; keep them steady.

1

2

3a

3b

3c

4

5

6

Making the base

7. You need a flat top before you start to pull out the base. Put your left hand on the exterior wall and place the side of your right hand (karate chop style) on top, so your little finger is in contact with the clay, flattening and compressing it down gently.

8. Using the thumb on your right hand, press toward the edge of the pot and wheel head to get rid of any excess clay that has been created while coning.

   You will know when the clay is centered by focusing on the middle point and walls. If this is off-center, then you need to keep repeating the above steps until you get it centered.

9. Once the ball of clay is looking centered, clasp your left hand over your right hand and wrist for support. Using your index and middle finger, find the center and press down to make a hole. Remember that your elbows need to be pressed down firmly on your thighs for support. Keep using water here to make it easier to press down. Push too far and you will end up with a hole in the base—leave it too thick and you will end up with a heavy pot (unless you want to make a foot ring; see page 96).

10. Test the thickness of your base by using a potter's needle. Stop the wheel and press the needle down into the base of your pot until it hits the wheel head. (10a)

    Place your finger on the base of the pot by the pin and lift up the pin to see how thick your base is. If it's looking too thick, then you can go back to step 9 and press down a little farther. Between 0.5 and 1 cm is a good thickness. Always leave more clay than you need. When you get around to wiring your pot off the wheel, a thin sheet of clay will be left behind due to the thickness of the wire. (10b)

Wheel speed: for steps 11–22, medium

11. Once you have the right base thickness, reduce the wheel speed and place your left hand over your right wrist. Slowly pull the base out in one straight line toward six o'clock, using the index and middle finger on your right hand—acting as a hook to open up the base. As you are pulling out, don't press down too much, because you don't want the base to get thinner. The diameter of the base is entirely dependent on the top diameter of your cylinder.

12. Start compressing the base to the wheel head with a small amount of pressure from the center out to three o'clock, finally touching the edge of the interior walls and back toward the center. This will even out the base and make it level.

    Spend some time doing this, especially if you are making larger pieces that have a wide surface area, such as plates. If you skip this step, you are quite likely to get cracks in the base of your pot during the drying and subsequent firing stages.

13. While the wheel is spinning, wet both hands and squeeze in from both sides of the exterior wall with equal amounts of pressure. This will cone the walls in, making it easier for you to pull the walls up in the next step.

The first pull

14. Make sure your walls always have a good coating of water. I find the best trick is to wet your sponge every time you are about to pull the walls up and to squeeze the water out on the rim of your pot so the water coats both the interior and exterior walls.

15

16

17

18

19

20

21

22

TIP
Creating height
Always pull the walls up in one straight line, keeping your hands between three o'clock and six o'clock (if right-handed). Keep your elbows firmly on your thighs for the first pull and try to resist the direction the wheel is pulling the clay, and go in the opposite direction.

15. On the exterior wall, you can either use a sponge, your knuckle, or your fingertips to pull the walls up. Personally I prefer using a sponge. Spin the wheel, then place your preferred option on the exterior wall at the base of your cylinder. Place the index and middle finger of your left hand on the interior of the pot toward the base. The sponge and your fingertips should be connecting like a magnet. You don't want the sponge to be disconnected from your fingertips. Try to imagine no wall in between. I usually connect my left thumb to the sponge for support.

16. Always start off at the base with each pull. With a small amount of pressure, pinch in from both sides and gradually pull up toward the rim and in toward the center.

17. Try not to think about height on the first pull. There will be a lot of clay toward the base of your pot, so apply the same amount of pressure from the base to the rim. The trick here is to even the walls out first, before you start on the second pull. Always concentrate on bringing the walls in toward the center.

The second and third pulls

18. Repeat step 16, but apply slightly more pressure at the base. To do this, I usually think of three words—push, pinch, and pull. From the base, push and pinch the exterior walls in toward the center of the wheel. At the same time, pinch from the interior and pull up toward the rim. This technique produces a ridge (as you can see in image 18), which will make your cylinder gain height. Applying too much pressure at the base will leave the walls too thin and provide no support.

    It's better to have a thicker base than a thick rim, since this can be trimmed (at the trimming stage). The rim is the most delicate part, so be really gentle when you reach the top and release really slowly.

If you find that your rim is not level, you can take a section off using a potter's knife. To do this, spin the wheel at medium speed, place the knife right against the pot and under the rim where it's uneven, then slowly push in. Stop the wheel once you have gone all the way through, and take off this layer (refer to step 7 on page 115).

19. The most important aspect here is to pull the clay wall toward the center—not outward. Essentially, you are making a conical shape. This is the best way to get the perfect cylinder shape. It will be difficult to straighten your walls into a cylinder if they are flaring out. If you find your walls are flaring out slightly, repeat step 13.

20. Every time you pull the walls up, compress the rim. Hold the thumb and index finger on your left hand around the rim and place your right finger on top (while the wheel is spinning) of the rim and gently compress.

Finishing

21. Straighten up the wall into a cylinder shape by using a rubber kidney, wooden rib, or old credit card on the exterior wall. While the wheel is spinning at medium speed, place your left hand inside the pot at the base and bring your fingers up against the interior walls, pressing against the card while doing so. Keep the card completely still and vertical.

22. When you are happy with the height and diameter of your pot and *before* taking it off the wheel, the water inside needs to be taken out so that your pot can dry evenly. I use a sponge on a stick for this. Spin the wheel and press gently toward the base of the pot to soak up all the water. Squeeze the water out into the jug you are using to throw with, so you can reuse it later.

Taking your pot off the wheel

Since I produce a lot of batch production work, I throw mainly on a wooden bat that attaches to my wheel head.

For students, this bat system is not always available on wheels, so I always teach the nudge-and-slide technique. This will work only if your base is narrow and you have made a small pot. If you are making a larger piece, it's best to throw on a bat (page 82), wire it through, and leave to dry on the bat.

Before attempting this technique, place a wooden board nearby to put your pot on after lifting it off the wheel.

23. Spin the wheel at medium speed. Make a little groove toward the base of your pot, using a wooden pointed tool—metal tools may scratch your wheel head. This groove will enable the wire to go through easily, so you can slide your pot off the wheel.

24. Take your foot off the pedal and sprinkle water all the way around your pot, but *not inside*. This acts as a sliding mechanism to take your cylinder off the wheel.

25. Using a potter's wire, place your hands inside the wire, with the wooden blocks on the outside. Point your index fingers up, then wrap them around the wire and press down with your thumbs on the wheel head.

26. Slide the wire through your pot. Do not at any point lift your thumbs or the wire up, since you will cut through the pot.

    On some occasions, the wire may catch the base of your pot and drag it to the edge of the wheel. If this happens, slowly bring the pot toward the edge of the wheel and push the wire down to the wheel pan.

27. Hold your thumbs up and place your two index fingers near the base of the cylinder and nudge the pot toward you until it meets the edge of the wheel head. The water will help the pot slide.

28. When your pot gets to the edge of the wheel head . . . (28a)

    . . . collect it with the rest of your fingers. (28b)

29. Carefully place your cylinder on a wooden board by slowly moving your fingers around the base of the pot. (29a)

    Try not to throw your piece down onto a wooden board as it may lose its shape. (29b)

REPETITION

Repetition is key to understanding the technique and art of throwing. It may seem like a laborious task, but it's the only way to understand how clay works.

Try not to be too precious over the first pots you make on the wheel. I spent hours in the ceramics workshop at university making hundreds of cylinders, all the time learning which hand movements, posture, and wheel speed work, and which don't.

It's hard to tell whether the walls of your cylinder are too thick or too thin when you're first starting out on the wheel. A little progression project would be to prepare your chosen clay as shown on pages 16–19 and divide into 10 x 14 oz. clay balls. Set yourself a measurement for the diameter and height of the piece you want to make. I threw the cylinder on page 62 to 3.5 in. diameter x 3.5 in. height (9 x 9 cm).

1.   Each time you make a cylinder and before you take it off the wheel, cut it in half with a wire to see the profile of the walls and base. To do this, repeat step 26 on page 70, but stop halfway and lift the wire up through your cylinder.

2.   Start placing your half cylinders next to each other on a wooden board. Before you begin to make more, inspect the one you have just made to see what needs better work.

The aim of this project is to really understand how repetition of certain hand movements and pressure points within the clay can make you feel more confident. There are a variety of ways to throw shapes on the wheel, and every potter has their own style, which makes it an interesting exercise to see what works for you. Try different hand movements; you may find it easier to use your knuckle on the exterior wall when pulling the walls up and not a sponge. Do what feels comfortable and you will soon get your own rhythm going.

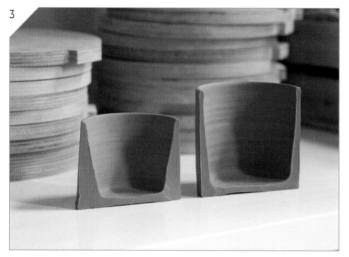

3

If your walls are showing more clay toward the base—like the left cylinder profile here—try to pinch in more at the base and grab the clay that has been left behind, but ease off the pressure as you lift up toward the rim.

The cylinder profile on the right in photo 3 is an example of an even wall and base, which, after a lot of repetition work, you should, one hopes, be achieving.

FUNCTION

If you look around your home, you'll notice that many objects derive from a cylinder shape but have a wide variety of functions. If you want to continue with the cylinder on the wheel, try experimenting with the overall finish and function. There will be certain aspects you'll need to practice on more, such as the rim if you want to make drinking cups. A thinner rounded rim is more enjoyable to drink from, as opposed to a really thick rim with a sharp edge.

Left: A variety of functions derived from one shape. The cylinders are all made with 400 g of white stoneware clay thrown to 3.5 in. diameter x 3.5 in. height (9 x 9 cm).

CYLINDER EXPERIMENTS

Once you feel more confident making cylinders, there are so many other forms to explore within the cylinder shape.

In all of these examples shown below, I used 14 oz. (400 g) of clay but still created a variety of forms. My first and second pull was a cylinder shape, and then the third and fourth pull I began to shape the cylinder in many different ways, from a tall vase to a short, wide sugar pot. If you are making a wide cylinder, remember to pull the base out more (step 11 on page 67). This experiment is a great way to see how many forms you can make using the same amount of clay. The main objective is to feel confident in pushing clay to its limits.

After experimenting with 14 oz. of clay, you can then move on to new shapes and sizes with a gradual increase in the weight of clay you are using. It's good practice to start off with small amounts of clay and then work your way up, rather than going full force into a 11 lb. (5 kg) planter, which I tried to do many times when I first started throwing.

Making a bowl

You may find that you have already made a bowl when learning to throw a cylinder. This is very common due to the natural force of the wheel, which can pull the walls out instead of in toward the center.

Throwing a bowl is very similar to throwing a cylinder, but there are a few aspects that you will need to consider before starting.

1. Depending on how large the bowl is, you may want to make it on a wooden bat, since it will be easier to take off the wheel (shown on page 82).
2. Will the walls be curved or straight?
3. Will the base have a foot ring?
4. Will the base be wide or narrow?

SMALL CURVED BOWL WITH A NARROW BASE

Prepare your clay first as shown on pages 16–19.

Measurements:

Clay: 14 oz. (400 g)

Thrown size: 6 in. diameter x 2.7 in. height (13 x 7 cm)

Wheel speed: for steps 1 to 5, medium

1. Follow steps 1–10 on pages 64–67. The thickness of your base is dependent on whether you will be turning a foot ring. If you are, make sure your base is approximately 0.6 in. (1.5 cm) or more thick. If not, then stick to approximately 0.2–0.4 in. (0.5–1 cm).

   Place your right hand over your left hand and start to pull out from the center in a curved line until you reach the rim. If you are making a bowl with a wider base, repeat step 11 on page 66.

2. Compress the interior shape by going back and forth from the center to the rim and then back to the center. Repeat these movements two or three times to get a curved interior.

   The first pull is very similar to the cylinder. Repeat this step but try to maintain a curved interior. For extra support, place your thumb on your left hand, next to the sponge on your right hand. At the same time, pinch in both sides and pull the walls up.

3. When pulling the walls up, make sure you always start from the base and continue up to finish at the rim. Try not to stop in between, since this may result in uneven walls. A bowl needs to have stability at the base, so it's always good to leave more clay at the base than toward the rim, since the base can easily be trimmed when you get to that stage.

4. Make sure you compress the rim each time you pull the walls up. Same as step 20 on page 69.

5. Second pull. Repeat step 18 on page 69. Push in from the exterior, pinch from both sides, and pull up toward the rim. Try to ease off the pressure as you reach the rim. The shape you want to make here is still a cylinder, but try not to cone in too much, since it will be difficult to bring the walls out into a bowl. Avoid pulling out straightaway when making a bowl, since you need a good amount of support at the base first. (5a)

   You may want to do a few more pulls before you shape the bowl. If you are going to do this, be wary of how thin your walls become. If they are too thin, it will be difficult to pull them out in the next stage. (5b)

6. Starting from the base, use the pads of your left fingers to push the interior wall out toward the sponge on the exterior wall in a curved line gradually toward the rim. (6a)

   Connect your thumbs to the sponge. (6b)

7. Place a curved-edge metal, rubber, or wooden kidney inside your bowl to shape and compress the clay at a curved angle. Do this really slowly with not too much pressure. This is a great way to get the interior of your bowl curved in a way your fingertips may not be able to achieve.

   Always remember that the interior is just as important as the exterior in anything you make on the wheel.

8. You can also use the same kidney on the outside of the bowl. Keep doing this, watching the internal shape more than the external.

   Soak up any water that has been left inside your bowl with a sponge.

9. Get rid of any excess clay at the base with a pointed wooden tool. Do not worry about how the edges of your base look at this stage, since they can be trimmed as shown on page 97.

10. Place water around your bowl, ready to nudge and slide off. Repeat steps 24–29 from pages 70–71.

6a

6b

7

9

8

10

Right: Profile section of two thrown bowls. The bowl on the left has been thrown with a thick base for a foot ring, and the right shows a thinner base since this style will not have a foot ring. Practice the repetition exercise on page 73 with the bowl shape and cut in half to see the wall thickness. Gradually build up the weight of clay you are using for larger bowls and wider bases.

POTTERY WHEEL BAT

When making batch production work or larger pieces on the wheel, I use a wooden bat that connects to my wheel head. My wheel didn't have this feature when bought, but I carefully drilled two holes into the wheel head and attached two metal pins so I could place wooden bats to throw on and then easily take them off for my work to dry. (1)

I have a variety of sizes of wooden bats in my studio to suit the range of products I make. I find this extremely useful for repetition work, and it means that my pieces are less likely to distort when taking off the wheel, since I can lift the wooden bat off the pins and place another on the wheel, ready for the next piece. (2)

If you do not have pins on your wheel, you can make your own clay bat to attach wooden boards to. If you are making your own wooden bat, the wood needs to be water resistant and not too thin, since they can warp if not dried properly.

The bat you use doesn't have to be made from wood; there are a variety of materials available such as plaster or plastic. However, I would recommend using wood, since it absorbs the moisture in the clay and aids drying.

Using a wooden bat

For a 12 in. (30 cm) diameter bat, you will need approximately 2.2–3.3 lb. (1–1.5 kg) of clay.

Wheel speed: for steps 1–2, fastest

1. Start by centering the ball of clay the same way as the methods shown on pages 64–67.

   Once it is centered, you need to push with your right hand or even use a rolling pin (while the wheel is spinning) on the top to flatten it down to create a clay pancake.

2. You can also use a sponge to help you pull out the clay even more. Start from the center and pull out toward the edges of the wheel. Make sure the top is level and flat. Aim for approximately 0.4 in. (1 cm) thickness.

Wheel speed: for steps 3–6, medium

3. Start making grooves within the pancake—this acts as a suction mechanism for the clay to attach to the wooden bat (3a–b).

4. Place your wooden bat on top of the clay pancake and spin the wheel gently to see if the bat is centered. Move it around slightly until it is fully centered, and then stop the wheel. Press the bat down with your hands to secure it to the clay pancake underneath.

5. Press down gently on the wooden bat with a wet sponge while the wheel is spinning. You will soon feel whether the board is level, since the sponge will make a consistent line on the board with the water.

6. If you can see that the line is not consistent and has gaps where it hasn't touched the bat, then pat the board down farther in those areas.

After making work on the wooden bat, wire through the base *without* any water. Leave your work on the bat and carefully release the bat off the clay pancake, using a hook tool. Place another bat on top and repeat steps 4–6. Before repeating these steps, you can neaten the grooves you made on the pancake if need be.

3a

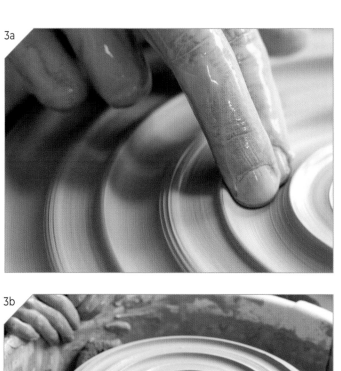

3b

4

5

6

TURNING AND FINISHING

TURNING AND FINISHING

In this chapter, instructions are with the wheel spinning counterclockwise.

For this stage in making, I tend to switch between two phrases: turning and trimming. They both have the same meaning but can be used interchangeably.

Turning is usually the second stage in making after you have thrown on the wheel or hand-built your piece. It can really transform your work. It gives you the chance to neaten and shape your form further by focusing on the exterior walls and the base. With certain shapes, this cannot be achieved at the throwing stage, since the clay will be too wet.

Turning works best when your work is "leather hard"—when the clay has dried to a consistency where it feels hard but still soft enough to be carved and trimmed using metal carving tools.

The drying time will all depend on the temperature in your studio. In winter months, my work can take up to three or four days for it to be ready to turn after throwing. In summer months, I can turn the next day. If I need to leave my thrown work for a few days until I'm ready to turn, I usually cover it up with a thin plastic sheet. This holds the moisture in, stopping the clay from hardening.

I have always thrown in a way where I do not need to spend too much time turning. The majority of my work has a simple flat base with a beveled edge to elevate it slightly from the surface it is sitting on. I find this fits in really well with my work aesthetic.

In this chapter, I demonstrate how to create a few simple but elegant finishes.

TOOLS

1. Credit card
2. Looped turning tools
3. Medium-firm rubber kidney (green)
4. Metal kidney
5. Potter's knife
6. Potter's needle
7. Soft rubber kidney (red)
8. Sponge

TURNING A FLAT BASE

This technique can be used for a variety of shapes. Before you start this process, pick up your pot when it is leather-hard, and feel the walls to gauge how much clay you are working with and how much you can trim away. Usually, this is thought out at the throwing stages; however, many people forget this stage and end up trimming away too much clay.

Wheel speed: medium throughout

1. Turn your piece upside down and place it in the center of the wheel. Press the pedal down slowly to see if it is centered. If it isn't, you can either stop the wheel and nudge it from one side, or you can keep the wheel spinning and gently tap it with one hand into the center. This method can be difficult to master, so be careful not to tap too hard, since you don't want to send your piece flying off the wheel. Use the circular markings on the wheel head to help center the piece.

2. When your piece is centered, get a small lump of clay and roll it into three small coils. I usually have a plastic container next to my wheel filled with scraps of the same clay I use to throw with but slightly harder in texture, so it doesn't stick to my leather-hard pot and the wheel.

3. Place the coiled pieces of clay evenly in a triangle around your pot. Hold the pot on the wheel head, using one hand, and individually press the clay down to the wheel and toward the exterior walls of your pot with your other hand. (3a)

   This secures the pot to the wheel head while you're trimming. Don't press too hard, since the rim of your pot can be very delicate. Keep the hand that's holding the pot steady, as it's stopping the pot from moving around. (3b)

4. Turning tools can be bought in all shapes and sizes. You can even make your own. I have a variety in my studio to suit the many different forms I make on the wheel. Make sure you hold your tool with a firm grip at the top, using your index finger, then place your thumb against the tool under your index finger.

5. Press down on the peddle at medium speed. Put the middle finger (or index finger) of your left hand on the base of the pot and hold the turning tool firmly toward the top end with your right hand. Slowly trim away the clay on the exterior walls. Make sure the wheel is spinning at medium speed. Your tool will be dragged around the pot if the wheel is spinning too slowly. (5a)

   If you are not holding your turning tool firmly against your pot while the wheel is spinning, then you can create jagged lines within your pot—this is called chattering. The key to trimming is to ease into it, by gently shaving away the clay and then applying more pressure.

   For more support while trimming, place your left thumb on top of your right thumb. Always spin the wheel first before putting any tool on your pot (5b).

   Keep in mind the direction the wheel is spinning in relation to how you hold and trim away the clay. Naturally, you want to follow the direction of the wheel, but always try to resist in the opposite direction. Hold the tool on your pot between three and six o'clock (if right-handed).

   It's important to hold the tool at the right angle so it can trim the clay easily. Turnings should fall off your pot in ribbons. Hold the tool at the angle that connects the sharp edge to the wall of your pot.

1

3b

5b

2

4

3a

5a

If your trimmings look very thin and short, then it may mean the clay is too dry. If your pot has dried too much, you can spray water on it or dunk it in water and let it dry slightly before putting it back on the wheel. Be careful with doing this, because if it's too dry and you dunk it in water, you run the risk of it cracking due to it being very fragile at this stage.

The profile edge should be in keeping with the overall shape of your pot. The most important aspect here is to keep reminding yourself how thick your walls and base are. You don't want to turn too much clay away, since your walls will get too thin and the pot may not survive the firing. Aim for an even wall consistency throughout the vessel.

6. The base of your pot may need some work to make it level. Spin the wheel, hold a turning tool—preferably a looped tool—gently in the center of the base and gradually trim out toward three o'clock (if the wheel is spinning counterclockwise). This movement should be slow and controlled.

7. I usually create a small dip in the middle of my base. I find that doing this helps it sit nicely on a flat surface without any wobble. After trimming your base, place a ruler or a straight-edge tool on the surface to test if there is a small gap between the clay and the ruler.

Making a chamfered edge on the base of your pot will elevate it from any surface it sits on. This technique is also important when you come around to glazing the piece. The elevated edge stops glaze from sticking directly to the kiln shelf.

I also find that a straight-sided pot with a sharp edge at the base is prone to getting knocked and chips easily.

8. Spin the wheel and hold a smaller turning tool at an angle and place it on the edge of your pot. You will need to have a steady hand here so the angle remains consistent.

9. Finish smoothing out the edges and base of the pot with a metal or rubber kidney. (9a, 9b)

Apply a thin coat of water with a sponge to give a smooth surface.

10. Stamp/sign the base of your pot.

11. Finished piece

Curved-edge base

Experiment with a range of curved and angular edges by holding the turning tool at a greater angle and by moving the tool around the edge of the pot rather than keeping it stationary. If the interior of your cylinder is curved, then the exterior should mimic this. I like to turn a curved edge on my mugs, since I feel it then sits really well in the hand and is very tactile.

Repeat all the steps on page 90–93 but make good use of a looped, curved turning tool and a flexible rubber kidney to shape the profile edge of your pot. Focus your turning at the top where the sides meet the base. (1)

Attaching your work to the wheel head without using coils
If you would like to work on the exterior walls from the base to the rim of your pot, you can attach your pot to the wheel head without using clay coils.

Sponge the rim of the pot and the wheel head with a small amount of water. Then turn your pot upside down and place in the center. Repeat step 1 on page 90 to get it centered, then gently tap it on the base to fully secure it. This method cannot be done if your pot is very thin and fragile. You will need to have it at the right clay consistency for it not to distort. (2)

To remove your pot from the wheel, gently hold all the sides and nudge it off the wheel slowly, either with the wheel spinning or keeping it stationary. (3)

If you have thrown shapes on the wheel that are difficult to turn when placed upside down—such as tall, narrow pieces— you may need to make a clay chuck. This device will allow you to place your shape inside the chuck and turn with ease. A clay chuck is used as an internal mold. It can either be made on the wheel then dried to leather-hard or you can use a fired piece/object.

TURNING A FOOT RING

A foot ring creates less contact between the base of your pot and the surface it sits on. It is a lovely feature to have and can also help when glazing your piece. The depth of your foot ring is entirely dependent on how much clay you have left at the base during the throwing stages.

Wheel speed: medium throughout

1. Repeat steps 1–3 on page 90.

2. While the wheel is spinning, apply a small amount of pressure and mark with a knife an inner circle on the base of your bowl. This is where you will trim the sides of the bowl to. The diameter of this inner circle is entirely dependent on the shape and size of your piece.

3. Trim the sides of the bowl until it meets the line you have just marked. Hold your turning tool at an angle to create a step, which will turn into the foot ring.

4. Once you have met the line, work more at a right angle to create a foot for the bowl.

5. Neaten and trim the sides. Try not to go too close to the three coils that are securing your pot to the wheel, since this may create further lines on your pot.

Repeat step 6 on page 93 to obtain a flat base.

6. Mark an inner circle on the base of your bowl (same as step 2), measuring approximately 0.2 in. (0.5 cm) from the outer circle. This will be your foot ring.

7. Start by trimming away the clay from the center out toward the line you have marked. Use both hands to hold the turning tool for a stronger grip. The fingers on my right hand are gripped toward one end of the tool, and my left hand has more grip toward the other end of the tool. Try not to put on too much pressure at the start. I use a straight edge loop tool for this, but you could use a curved loop tool instead.

8. Keep repeating step 7, making sure you are always starting from the center. At this stage, you want to make sure your movements are controlled and not too fast, since you could run the risk of taking away too much clay. You are aiming for a leveled inner foot.

   Keep checking the thickness of the foot ring you are trimming by tapping it in the center; if it feels springy or sounds hollow, do not trim any more, since you could potentially create a hole in the base.

9. Use a straight edge tool to neaten up the inside and outside edges.

10a

12

10b

10. Trim a beveled edge on the outside and inside of the foot ring. (10a–b)

11. Carefully remove the three coils from the wheel and lift your bowl off the wheel head. Use a sponge to soften the edges of the rim.

12. The finished piece

11

Making a handle

Handles can be made in a variety of shapes and sizes, although it can be challenging to get the right shape in order for it to feel comfortable to hold and drink from. Handles are usually attached after you have trimmed your pot.

I have tested many handle shapes over the years and have made many mistakes when trying to be too experimental. I have realized that a traditional, simple shape works best for my work aesthetic. The handle and main vessel of any mug should complement each other. With this in mind, I have always used the traditional pulling technique to make my handles, since this fits in well with the simple, finely thrown cylinders I make for the main body.

Everyone has a favorite mug at home, so use this for your research and ask yourself a few design questions. Why does it feel comfortable to hold? What is the size-and-shape ratio between the vessel and the handle? Is the handle placed toward the base of the vessel or toward the rim? Is it a wide handle or a thin one?

First, you need to work out the length of your handle.

Experiment with shapes and sizes by using a strip of paper and attaching it loosely to your trimmed cup. You can then choose which works best against the main vessel you have made. I have a handy sketch I use each time I shape my handles. I've marked the exterior profile of my mugs and drawn a handle to the shape I feel fits in well with the overall look.

I then get a strip of paper and measure it against the handle I have drawn, to determine the length of the handle I need to pull in the next stage.

1. Prepare the clay as shown on pages 16–19. Start by shaping a piece of clay (preferably the same clay you have used for the main vessel) into a rectangular block that has a point at one end. Hold this up high with one hand and have a bowl/jug of water underneath.

2. Wet your other hand and start to pull down toward the bowl of water.

3. Use the inside curve of your thumb and index finger to shape the clay and its sides.

4. Keep pinching and pulling down, using water as you work. Apply even pressure from the top part of the clay to the end. Try not to squeeze too much, since you don't want the handle to get too thin.

5. When you are happy with the length and thickness of the handle you have just pulled, place it carefully on a clean, flat wooden board. Now press your thumb on top of the handle and into the wooden board to release it. You can then repeat the steps above with the rest of the clay you have in your hand.

I usually make more handles than I need, so I can choose the best ones.

6. Leave the handles on the wooden board to dry slowly. Don't leave them for too long, since the next step is shaping, and if they are too dry, they will snap.

If you cannot see any fingerprint marks when picking your handles up from the board, they are (usually) ready for use at this stage. When they are ready, pick your handles up one by one and shape each around the sketch drawing you have made. I find this drawing gives me a better indication of what my handle will look like, rather than guessing or making it up as I go along.

7. Cut the handle where it meets the outline of your cup, and reclaim the excess clay from the pieces you have cut away. I prefer cutting the handle this way, since I often find that the top part of the handle is thinner than the bottom (when pulling), so using the middle section to cut works perfectly.

8. Keep all the shaped handles on a wooden board, ready to be attached to your main vessel.

9. Handles should vary in size to be in proportion with your main vessel.

The handle and main vessel of your cup should be of a similar clay consistency for both pieces to attach together securely. This is usually at leather-hard consistency.

If your handles are too dry, they will not attach to your main vessel very well and may result in developing fatal cracks when drying.

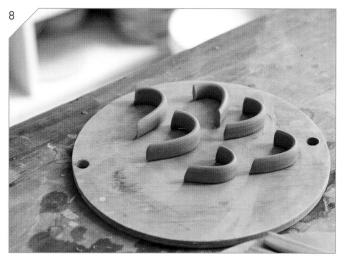

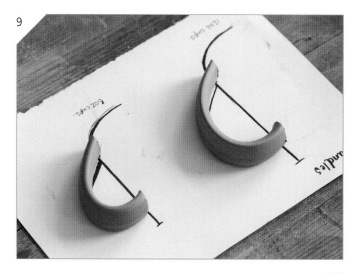

10a

10b

11a

11b

12

13

14a

14b

15

10. Position the handle on your cup to where you want it, and mark gently with a knife, where it will be joined. (10a–b)

11. Using either a potter's knife or serrated kidney, cross-hatch your cup and both ends of the handle. (11a–b)

12. Dab water or slip on the ends of the handle and the cup where you have just made the markings.

13. Place the handle on the cup where you have marked. Apply a little pressure to secure both joints.

14. Smooth joints with your thumb and a sponge, making sure the handle is connected well. (14a–b)

15. The completed mug

When you have finished attaching the handle, place a plastic sheet over your mug (or mugs) so they can dry slowly and evenly. If you dry your mugs too quickly, the handles may show signs of cracks within the joints, which will affect the following firing and glazing stages.

GLAZING

GLAZING

Color is so important to me, and it shows across my range. I love using a variety of colors throughout my work that can suit a whole range of interior settings. Not only can it enhance food and drink, but the sensory effects caused by vibrant glazes and the reaction from customers are what really extends my passion.

I also love neutral colors in many potters' work. I aspire to the simplicity of really showcasing the clay more than the glaze, but I can't deny that whenever I make anything on the wheel, I tend to always think about color first and how my excitement can be transferred to the consumer. It enhances my mood and brings me joy, and I honestly feel it can do the same in anyone's home.

There are three main ingredients that make up a glaze: alumina, silica, and flux. Using these ingredients in different mixes and quantities produces a variety of surfaces, textures, and colors, which makes glazing a fascinating process, although slightly terrifying to some. It's another side of pottery that has its challenges but can be extremely rewarding.

Glazes are usually applied to work after bisque firing. Your work will then go back into the kiln and fired to a temperature relating to your clay and glaze recipe. Whether you are purchasing store-bought glazes or making your own glaze, make sure you check the firing range within that recipe. This must relate to the firing temperature in your kiln program: you cannot put a low-fired clay and glaze within a high-fired firing schedule.

During my fourth year at university, I worked for ceramicist Louisa Taylor, which consisted mainly of mixing hundreds of glaze tests. This was a definite starting point for my love of glazes and color. The ceramics workshop at university had a fantastic range of materials we could experiment with. I spent endless hours there—I also spent endless hours trying to figure out why things didn't work or go to plan.

The main purpose of using glaze in my work is to enhance its function, so food and drink can be served inside, as well as to bring a variety of characteristics and aesthetics across my range. It is vital that my glazes are food safe and stable. You must test any glaze you put on your work before selling it as a food-safe product. Tests can be done in your studio or you can send your work off to a laboratory. There are a wide range of resources available in different countries for these tests. You absolutely must not use any glaze that contains lead or barium for tableware.

The lemon test

A very simple food-safe home test is to squeeze a small segment of lemon onto a glazed surface (after firing). Leave overnight and check the next day to see if the acidity from the lemon has leached onto the glazed surface or discolored the glaze in any way. If it has, then your glaze is not food safe and your recipe will need to be modified/changed. If you are unsure of the materials that are being used in commercial glazes, it's always best to check with the supplier. Same goes with glazes made in your studio; you should always research each raw ingredient you use.

Commercial glazes can easily be bought from pottery suppliers, but If you have the resources, equipment, and space to mix your own, then I would definitely recommend experimenting. It can be a lengthy process to begin with, but once you have the right setup and understanding of materials, you will be able to produce a wide range of results that will be a lot cheaper than buying commercial glazes.

TEST TILES

Test tiles have many functions: they can be used to test clay bodies, glazes, underglazes, slip, and surface patterns. Test tiles will be used for this chapter to document glazes on the same clay body I use throughout my work; namely, white stoneware. It is really useful to see a glaze on a test tile before applying it to a larger form. Document your test tiles well by keeping notes on the back of your tile and in a sketchbook. I usually have a separate sketchbook in my studio for glaze recipes. There have been many times when I've made a test glaze and forgotten to write notes and then later regretted it.

Test tiles can be made in a variety of ways and in any shape you like. Making vertical and horizontal tiles can be very useful because glazes can look completely different when applied to a vertical wall of a pot, as opposed to a flat surface such as a plate. You may discover you have a runny glaze only when trying it out on a vertical test tile.

Flat

Flat hand-built test tiles are made by rolling out a slab of clay the same as steps 1–3 on page 44, and preferably the same thickness as the work you make either on the wheel or when hand-building.

Using a cookie cutter or a potter's knife, cut the shape and size you want. My flat test tiles are usually 1.6 in. wide x 2.4 in. high (4 x 6 cm). You can also make a hole toward the top of your tile to hang on a wall after firing. I have a metal sheet in my studio that I use to place all my test tiles on. After the glaze firing, I glue a magnet on the back of the test tile so it can easily attach to the metal sheet. This allows me to move them around freely in case I want to see what color combinations work or don't work together.

Vertical

Using the same technique as the flat, you can hand-build a vertical test tile. Roll out a slab of clay and cut out a rectangle for the main body and a smaller rectangle for the foot. Score the edge of the main body test tile and the area on the foot you will be joining it to. Apply water on the scored area and connect these two pieces (see below).

HAND-THROWN TEST TILES

Vertical

I recommend practicing your throwing skills with larger amounts of clay first before you tackle this technique on the wheel, since you will need approximately 5.5 lb. (2.5 kg) of clay.

You will need to use a pottery wheel bat as shown on pages 82–85. The bat I'm using here is 11.9 in. (30 cm) in diameter. It is also important to throw these test tiles to the same thickness as you intend to throw your pieces.

Wheel speed: steps 1–4 fastest

1. Prepare your clay as shown on pages 16–19. Centre your clay on the wheel as show on page 64 and flatten the top down into a pancake, using either the side of your hand, your fist, or a sponge, or even applying pressure using a rolling pin. The rolling pin will flatten the clay easily and will have less strain on your wrists. Try to work slowly and keep the clay centered.

2. Find the center and press right down to the bat (creating a hole), using a sponge or your fingers.

3. Pull out the base bit by bit until the exterior walls are 0.8 in. (2 cm) away from the edge of the wooden board. The exterior diameter of the rim should be approximately 10 in. (26 cm).

4. Leave a 1.2–1.6 in. (3–4 cm) wide x 0.2–0.4 in. (0.5–1 cm) high step, before pulling the walls up. This will act as a foot for the tile to stand up straight.

Wheel speed: steps 5–11 medium

5. Gradually pull the walls up the same way as making a cylinder on page 68. The height is dependent on how much clay you have to work with and how thin your walls are usually in your work.

6. Leave a small step (0.4 in) on the outside of your wall, toward the base, so the weight of your tile can be counterbalanced.

7a

7b

8

9

10

11a

7. If your rim is uneven, use a potter's knife to carefully cut into the rim while the wheel is spinning. (7a)

    Remove this layer. (7b)

8. Straighten the exterior wall, using a straight edge tool such as a kidney or old credit card.

9. Soften and compress the rim by placing your left thumb and forefinger on the interior and exterior wall of the rim, and position your forefinger on your right hand on top. The rim of your test tiles should mimic the overall look of your rims on your pots.

10. The finished piece

11. Wire through your piece and leave it to dry to leather-hard. Spin the wheel at medium speed and cut the inner step down with a potters knife to approximately 0.8 in. (2 cm) from the interior wall. (11a–b)

12. At the leather-hard stage, use a potter's knife to slice through the walls to make your test tiles. You can either do this by eye or mark on the rim where you want to cut before this stage.

Lift each tile off the wheel and let it dry completely before the bisque firing. Make sure you fire these to the same bisque temperature as you will be using when you make your work.

11b

12

BASE GLAZE

Experimenting with a base glaze first will make the glazing process a little easier to begin with. Base glazes have no colorants in them; they act as a neutral color that you add oxides or stains to. My studio glazes consist mainly of two base glazes: shiny white and a shiny transparent. I mix big batches of each and then divide this into smaller buckets, where I add oxides and stains to create my colored glazes. I find this is the best way for my studio production in terms of space and time. I wouldn't want to have a different base glaze for each colored glaze, since this would be very time consuming to make.

In this chapter, I demonstrate how effective it can be working with one base glaze mixed with oxides and stains to produce a variety of colors. For the eight-glaze recipes on pages 124–125, I have used Linda Bloomfield's glossy transparent glaze (as the base glaze) originating from Stephen Murfitt's *The Glaze Book* (p. 251). Linda has modified this recipe slightly, and it can be found in her *Colour in Glazes* book (p. 108)

Oxides and stains are raw powders made up of a variety of properties that are available from a wide range of pottery suppliers. Oxides are natural metal elements that are ground to a powder. Stains are less natural, but more refined and stable. They are made up of metal elements mixed with dyes and ground to a powder form. They are also more predictable when understanding what color they will look like when fired.

Mixing a glaze is the simplest part to glaze making. It's the not knowing and the "what ifs" that make it a daunting process. Make sure you write each step down and any little changes you may have made to a glaze before anything goes into the kiln. It can be very frustrating when you take your pieces out of the kiln and ask yourself, "How did I get that color?"

It's best to test glaze recipes on bisqued tiles, using the clay you intend to work with and the temperature you are going to fire your work to. (1)

For any glaze test you make, the total ingredients will need to be equal to 100 g. Each number below relates to the percentage and is measured in grams.

Glossy transparent base glaze recipe (2)

Heat range:	2,264°F–2,300°F / 1,240°C–1,260°C (Cone 6-8) Oxidized

Ingredients:

Potash feldspar:	34
Calcium borate frit:	14 (calcium borate frit can be changed to borax frit)
Whiting :	11
China clay:	13
Quartz:	23
Dolomite :	5

1

2

MAKING GLAZES
3.5 OZ. (100 G) GLAZE TEST

Before making a large batch of glaze, It's always best to make a small glaze test to see if it is compatible with your clay.

Make sure all of your ingredients are laid out in front of you before you begin. When working with raw ingredients and oxides, a respiratory mask *must* be worn. Without realizing, dust from raw ingredients can easily become airborne from making glazes and generally working with clay in your studio.

This is a health risk and should not be ignored, since exposure to these conditions over a long period of time may cause silicosis, which damages your lungs.

Raw ingredients should be kept in airtight containers and labeled clearly for easy access. I use two different sized scoops for measuring and a small spoon for the ingredients that need smaller quantities, such as oxides and stains.

Tools
1. Brush: to mix ingredients together
2. Digital scales: two types, one for larger quantities and one that measures from 0.1 g for smaller quantities
3. Plastic tubs: to weigh out ingredients
4. Respiratory mask: essential
5. Rubber kidney: to press ingredients through the sieve
6. Sieve: small test sieve, 80–100 mesh
7. Spoon: to measure small amounts
8. Test tiles: bisqued for glaze application

Put on your respiratory mask before making your glaze. Have your recipe in front of you and the materials ready. All of your raw ingredients should add up to 3.5 oz. (100 g). Oxides and colorants are an added percentage.

1. Weigh out approximately 2–2.4 oz. (60–70 g) of water in a small container (#1) and place that to one side.

2. Weigh your first ingredient on the scales into another small container, #2 (2a) then tip that into container #1. (2b)

   Placing your ingredients into water first will reduce dust particles.

   Weigh out your second ingredient into container #2 and then transfer it to container #1. Keep doing this process until all the raw ingredients have been measured and placed in container #1.

   Stir all the ingredients together. The majority of stoneware glazes I use are mixed to a creamy consistency. Let this mixture settle for between five and ten minutes. Some raw ingredients react differently from others when water is added. You may need to add more water to some of your glazes, but less in others.

3. Pour container #1 into an empty container through a small test sieve. Use a brush or rubber kidney to make sure all the ingredients are pressed through the mesh. Repeat this two more times so all ingredients are fully mixed.

4. Apply the glaze to a test tile. If your glaze is mixed to the right consistency, it should dry instantly on your test tile and turn into a powdery form.

1

3

6

2a

4

5. If you are dipping a flat test tile into your glaze, make sure you wipe off any glaze from the back of the tile. If you leave any glaze on the back, it will stick and fuse to your kiln shelf once fired.

6. Write on your test tiles with an underglaze pencil the glaze you have used. Or make your own solution with iron oxide mixed with a small amount of water, and paint the recipe on the back.

2b

5

MAKING A LARGER BATCH OF GLAZE

Tools

1. Bowl
2. Digital scales
3. Respiratory mask: essential
4. Rubber kidney
5. Scoops: for measuring
6. Sieve: large sieve at 80–100 mesh
7. Spoon: for measuring small oxides and stains
8. Test tiles
9. Wooden sticks

If you have already made a glaze test tile with your base glaze and are happy with the results after firing, you can multiply all your ingredients to make a bigger batch to add colorants to.

For example, below I have multiplied each ingredient from page 117 by thirty to make a 6.6 lb. (3 kg) batch of the glossy transparent glaze recipe:

Potash feldspar	1.020 kg
Calcium borate frit	420 g
Whiting	330 g
China clay	390 g
Quartz	690 g
Dolomite	150 g

1. Two large buckets are useful for transferring and sieving ingredients. Measure out your ingredients the same as in steps 1–2 on page 120. Be aware that the water content varies throughout different glazes: I usually add less water than needed at first. It's easier to add more water than to take away. After adding all ingredients to water, stir it before leaving everything to settle overnight. Mix the next day. You will find that it's a lot easier to sieve after being left overnight. If you can't wait, then let your ingredients settle for at least a couple of hours.

2. Place a sieve with two wooden sticks (same thickness) on top of a wide bucket or bowl. Pour the glaze through the sieve bit by bit, using a rubber kidney (the same as in step 3 on page 120).

   Sieving two to three times will combine all ingredients together well, making sure there are no lumps of raw ingredients left in the bucket. I use a 80-mesh sieve to start and then move onto a 100-mesh sieve. There are a variety of grades you can get, but these two sieves have worked very well for me over the years.

3. I have always tested glaze thickness by eye with the dipping test. After mixing the glaze, dip your fingers into the glaze bucket. When lifting them out, if the glaze pours off and you can see the lines around your knuckles through the glaze, this is a good indication that the thickness is right. If the glaze falls off your fingers completely, it means that the glaze is too thin. My glazes are usually a creamy consistency.

You may find that the amount of water you use will differ across your glaze recipes due to the raw ingredients used within each recipe. Some glazes will look and feel thicker than others. Make sure you thoroughly test and take note of how much water you have used to produce consistent results. If you do decide that your glaze is thin, leave the glaze to one side and allow it to settle. You can then remove / siphon off the excess water.

ADDING COLORANTS TO THE BASE GLAZE

When adding colorants, you will need 3.5 oz. (100 g) base glaze to start with.

These eight colored glazes have all been made using 100 g of glossy transparent base glaze (recipe on page 117), plus a stain or oxide.

If you would like to use the base glaze identified in this chapter but want to experiment with other stains and oxides, just make sure they can fire between 2,264°F–2,300°F (1,240°C–1,260°C).

Apricot—3.5 oz. base + 0.1 oz. (3 g)
High-fire tango-orange stain

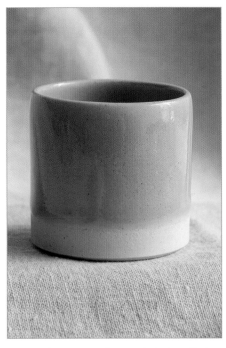

Aqua mint—3.5 oz. base + 0.035 oz. (1 g)
Copper carbonate

Emerald—3.5 oz. base + 0.070 oz. (2 g) Copper carbonate

Pink rose—3.5 oz. base + 0.053 oz. (1.5 g) Rutile + 0.141 oz. (4 g) tin oxide

Vanilla—3.5 oz. base + 0.070 oz. (2 g) High-fire canary-yellow stain

Ocean blue—3.5 oz. base + 0.035 oz. (1 g) Cobalt oxide

Plum—3.5 oz. base + 0.1 oz. (3 g) Maroon stain

White—3.5 oz. base + 0.28 oz. (8 g) Tin oxide

1. With your larger batch of base glaze made, distribute 3.5 oz. into small cups or containers. This acts as 100% base glaze, which you can then add your colorants to.

   Weigh the oxides and stains separately and add them individually to the cups. You can use a paper to weigh your colorants on a digital scale; alternatively, a small lid from a container works too. (1a–1b)

2. Stir well and leave to settle.

   Make sure you use a test sieve two or three times to fully mix in the colorants within the glaze. Same as step 3 on page 120.

   Glaze a test tile and repeat steps 4–6 on pages 120–121.

If you are happy with a particular colored glaze test after firing and want to make a larger batch, make sure you multiply the colorant with the same amount you have multiplied each ingredient in the base glaze.

1a

1b

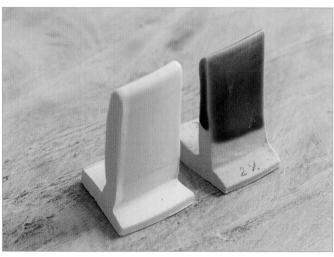

Right: An example of the before and after emerald-green glaze recipe with 2% copper carbonate (recipe on page 125)

LINE BLEND

Line blending is a great technique used to test a variety of percentages within a selected oxide or stain.

The image above shows four percentage variations of copper carbonate mixed with the glossy transparent base glaze recipe described on page 117.

Add in equal measures as you build up a colorant in your base glaze for ease of measuring. Then, when you eventually want to make a bigger batch of the glaze, it will be straightforward to multiply your ingredients.

1. Pour 3.5 oz. of the base glaze into one cup.

2. Add 0.5% (grams) copper carbonate (or your chosen oxide or stain) to your base glaze cup. Mix and sieve. Dip a test tile into that mixture and label it as 0.5%.

3. Repeat step 2 by adding another 0.5% of copper carbonate to the same base glaze cup. This will mean that you now have 1% copper carbonate on your test tile.

4. Keep adding 0.5% copper carbonate to the same cup while making sure you repeat step 2 with mixing, sieving, and labeling your test tiles.

It's entirely up to you how far you want to go with the oxide or stain you are using, but I would recommend not using more than 2%–3% for tableware glazes.

Glaze application

Applying glaze to your work usually happens after bisque firing. Raw glazing can be applied to unfired clay, but this can produce numerous problems. If you are glazing a bisqued piece and have an accident, it's very easy to scrape and wipe the glaze off so you can start again. With raw glazing, there is no room for error.

There are many techniques used to apply glaze on bisqueware. Glaze can be poured, dipped, brushed, splattered, layered, sprayed, or even painted. It all depends on the type of glaze you are using and the effect you want to achieve. Some glazes are not compatible with certain application methods, but it's always good to experiment on a test tile first.

I use the pour-and-dunk method throughout my work. I find it works best for me, since I make a lot of batch production work, so working this way is effective on a larger scale.

Before applying any glaze to your pieces, make sure your bisque ware is sanded and cleaned. A flexible diamond sanding pad is a great sanding tool and is best used with water to reduce dust. You can get different grades of diamond pads to suit your clay body. I start off with a coarse grade, then move on to a much-finer grade that makes the surfaces lovely and smooth. I also sand the base of my pieces when they come out of the glaze firing.

After sanding your pieces, make sure they are cleaned well with water and are completely free from dust. Glaze will not adhere to your piece if it is wet, so it's really important to let your bisqueware dry completely before applying the glaze.

The main rule for glazing your pieces is to not leave any glaze on the base of your pot before placing it in the kiln. If there is glaze on the base, it will melt and stick to the kiln shelf, which will ruin your pot completely—and your kiln shelf.

Make sure the glaze in your bucket is mixed well before using. You can use a stick or an electric mixer to stir the glaze, but I find mixing with a toilet brush is the best method, and you can leave it in the bucket when not in use. It is important to mix your glaze properly before applying, since some components in a glaze like to settle at the base of the bucket. If you don't mix your glaze properly, it can really affect the color and overall finish of your work—not necessarily in a good way.

GLAZING A PIECE WITH AN UNGLAZED BOTTOM HALF SECTION

This has to be my favorite glaze finish across all my work. I love the contrast between the shiny glaze surface next to the raw, textured, unglazed clay.

1. Fill a small jug with glaze and hold it with one hand and the piece you are about to glaze in your other hand (I prefer to hold my work with my left hand). You want as little contact as possible with your fingers while holding the piece, since it helps when dunking into the glaze.

2. Pour glaze inside your pot right up to the rim and pour out straight away, not too fast but not too slow either. You are likely to obtain drips on the exterior of your pot if you pour out too slowly—though you can remove them before the next step. (2a)

   Another technique for applying interior glaze is to pour a small amount of glaze inside and then gently rotate your pot around while slowly pouring out the glaze. (2b)

3. Immediately dunk your pot into the bucket of glaze to your desired height and hold for a few seconds so the glaze can adhere to the pot. Lift the pot out of the glaze bucket and hold it at an upside-down angle to allow the drips to pour out into the glaze bucket. You can also rotate your cup so the last few drips are evenly placed around the rim.

Bisque ware is porous after firing, so it won't take much time for the glaze to dry and settle into a powder form. It all depends on the thickness of your piece. If your glaze is taking a long time to dry, then you may need to change the components slightly in your recipe, or it could be that your walls are thin.

If you are glazing your piece a different color on the exterior wall from what it is on the interior wall, it's best to wait a day before applying glaze to the exterior. This is so the glaze can adhere to the walls and dry inside first.

Drips on the interior or exterior can be fettled off. If you have made a mistake while glazing that you cannot rectify, the glaze can be scraped off your pot and into your glaze bucket and reused.

GLAZING THE INTERIOR OF A PLATE

This is the plate shown on page 42.

1. Hold the plate with one hand, making sure you grip the outside rim but not the interior. Pour the glaze inside and swirl it around so it meets the inside rims. (1a)

   Then pour out on one side (at one angle), letting the drips pour out into the glaze bucket. (1b)

2. Scrape any glaze that has poured on the exterior of the plate into the glaze bucket, and wipe the exterior walls and base clean.

1a

1b

2

Glazing a whole piece

This technique is for pieces that are fully covered with glaze, with the exception of the base.

1. Apply wax-resist emulsion to the base of your piece, either by holding it or placing it on a wheel and brushing it on while the wheel is spinning at a low speed. Wax up to the beveled edge on the pot. If you do not have this edge, then make sure you wax 0.02–0.12 in. (2–3 mm) from the base up to the exterior wall. If the glaze is in contact with the kiln shelf, it will fuse to it when fired and ruin your piece.

   Wax emulsion can be commercially bought. It will help when dipping your piece in the glaze bucket since the glaze will resist the waxed area, meaning you won't need to further scrape off the glaze on the base of your pot before placing it in the kiln. Wax will burn off during the glaze firing. You could skip this part and not wax the base but later scrape and remove the glaze after you have applied it on your piece.

2. Metal tongs can be bought from many pottery suppliers, and are used to eliminate fingerprint marks. Grip your pot with one part of the tong on the exterior and the other on the interior.

3. Fully submerge your pot in the glaze bucket and swirl it around so the whole pot is coated.

4. Lift the pot out of the bucket and let all the drips slide off. Hold the pot at an angle instead of shaking it around, since otherwise you may lose your grip on the tongs.

   Carefully place your pot on a flat surface and release the tongs from the pot. Smooth over the four small dots with your fingertips where the tong has gripped the pot.

5. Wipe off any glaze from the base of the pot.

GLAZING A LAYERED BOWL

Layering glazes can produce beautiful effects and add a whole new dimension to the glaze. Experiment first on test tiles, since you will soon find out that some oxides / raw ingredients are more powerful than others, so layering these on top of a weaker oxide will not have any effect. It is important to keep note of the first layer and the overlapping color. There have been many times I haven't written this down and have been left very confused with which glaze I used first. The thickness of the glaze will also affect the overall look. There is a lot of trial and error with this process, but it's definitely worth experimenting.

1. Wax the base, making sure sure there is at least 0.02–0.12 in. (2–3 mm) from the base to the exterior wall of the pot.

2. Hold the pot with one hand, using just fingertips, and dip the pot into the glaze bucket more than halfway. (1)

3. Pull out and hold at an angle to remove drips. Let this dry fully before glazing the other side.

4. Hold the glazed side and dip the other half into another bucket of glaze, making sure it overlaps. Pull your pot out of the bucket slowly at an angle to ensure the drips are removed, before placing it on your work surface. (2)

5. Sponge off any glaze that has gathered at the base.

FETTLING

Fettling can be used in many areas of pottery, but for glazing, it is often used to remove glaze drips and mishaps. Carefully fettle away glaze drips, using a knife, and then smooth over using your fingertips. Try not to press too firmly when fettling, since you can potentially scrape too much glaze away. Anything you scrape away can be put back in the same glaze bucket to stir and use again. (3)

FIRING

FIRING
KILNS

There are a variety of kilns you can purchase, such as electric, gas fired, and top and front loaders, which come in a variety of shapes and sizes (and prices!). Make sure you are fully confident of the electricity supply in your workshop before purchasing. Kilns can be an expensive piece of equipment for your studio, but if looked after well they can last a very long time. Throughout this chapter, all explanations and techniques will relate to electric kilns.

A few points to consider before purchasing a kiln:

- Check the electricity supply in your studio and the building you are working in. Don't forget that while your kiln is on, there may be other equipment being used at the same time; this might overload the system.

- What is the firing temperature range of your work?

- How much work are you producing? Calculate the interior space of the kiln you are looking into, in relation to the amount of work you can fit inside.

- Are you looking for oxidation or reduction firing?

- Would you prefer a top loader or front loader?

- Manufacturing country. It's worth looking into this properly, because if you need new elements or spare parts, it will probably be easier to purchase these if the kiln is made in the country you are in. Occasionally, there are delays in transit and purchasing for overseas orders, and possibly additional customs duties or taxes.

- The space your kiln is in needs to be well insulated from floors, walls, and ceilings.

- Check the space around your kiln. You need *at least* 11.9 in. (30 cm) from your kiln to the wall for heat to flow evenly.

- Check if there are any regulations within your building for equipment this size.

- Finally, check the access for getting the kiln into your studio before purchasing.

Health and safety

Kilns should be placed in a well-ventilated room, since they can produce harmful fumes while on. If you are using wax-resist on your pieces, this will burn off during firing, but be aware that this can produce very unpleasant gases.

The flooring your kiln sits on should be noncombustible. Concrete or tiled flooring work best with the amount of heat kilns can produce. Any other material such as carpet or wood is a potential fire hazard.

Please read the manufacturer's instructions carefully before installing. I highly recommend a qualified electrician to install your kiln. Trying to install it yourself may result in further issues and time wasted.

Kilns may seem overwhelming for a first-time potter, but as long as you fully read the instructions and get qualified advice on electricity and ventilation, they are safe and will last a long time if looked after well.

Kiln controller

A controller is usually supplied with a kiln that connects to a pyrometer/thermocouple, which sits inside the kiln. The controller will display the temperature in the kiln, and it will also have functions that relate to ramps within the temperature range of your firing. You can also use pyrometric cones as a manual alternative to test the temperature in your kiln.

Manufacturers may preprogram the controller to make it easier for you to manage. However, every glaze/clay/finish you want to achieve may need these preprogrammed settings changed. This is easily done by changing the ramps and temperature, but make sure you keep a note on what you are changing. Once you have set a program on the controller and start your kiln, this will heat up the elements inside and maintain the firing program throughout.

Kiln elements

The elements are metal coils inside your kiln that heat up to your set temperature and will turn your greenware into ceramic. They are very important and should be looked after well. They will need changing every so often, depending on the kiln and the amount of firings you do. (1)

Indications that elements need changing are:

- A change of appearance/slant to one side (2)

- Your glazed pieces are not coming out the way they should, which could mean the kiln may not have reached the designated temperature.

- The firing time takes longer than expected. Old, worn-out elements will take longer to heat up to your set temperature.

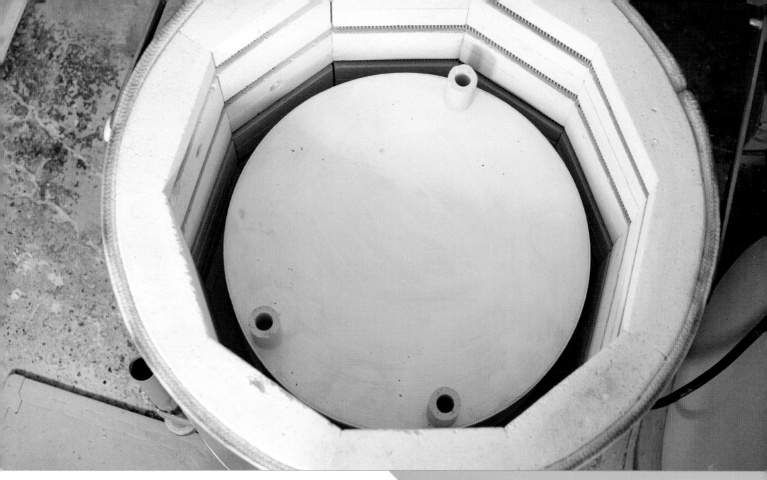

Kiln shelves and props

Usually, there is one shelf that sits at the bottom of a kiln. Underneath this shelf there should be at least three small kiln props in a triangular arrangement. You should follow this procedure as you begin to add more props and shelves in the kiln. Your shelves will be evenly proportioned this way, and it will prolong the life of each one. Kiln shelves may distort over time due to the extreme heat in the kiln, so it is vital to place your kiln props and shelves correctly.

Kiln props can come in different shapes and sizes. It's best to get a variety of heights to suit your work and to avoid unnecessary space wastage in the kiln. Being space savvy within your kiln will be the best way to reduce firings, electricity costs, and energy supply.

Bone-dry vases next to greenware tumblers

BISQUE FIRE

The first firing is called bisque/biscuit firing. This is where the chemical compounds within the clay are burned off at temperatures ranging between 1,742°F and 1,940°F (950°C–1,060°C). Moisture is released from the clay during the firing to produce a porous clay, which will allow for an easier glaze application.

Your pieces need to be completely dry before putting them in the kiln for bisque fire. In pottery terms, we call this "bone dry." This is monitored by touch and color. Being patient with timings and knowing when your piece has fully dried are vital in this stage of pottery. If you spot any faults within your pieces before bisque fire, then it's best to reclaim this clay because after the first firing the clay cannot be reworked.

A bisque fire should be programed to start off slowly to allow all the moisture to escape at an even rate. Heat and moisture escape through a vent hole on either the side or top of your kiln. If heat rises too quickly and if there is any moisture within the clay, this will turn into steam and may cause the clay to burst or explode.

When the kiln has reached temperature, it will need to have a soak period; this is when the controller sets a hold time for the whole kiln to reach temperature. If the soak period is short, you may find that parts of your kiln have not reached temperature, which will affect the glaze and clay consistency in your pieces. This is very common, so make sure your soaking period is at least twenty minutes. This soaking period will differ from time to time depending on your glaze and clay body. After reaching temperature, the cooling period should be slow to allow your pots to get back to room temperature at an even rate.

Make sure you leave out the bung that fits inside the vent hole during the first stages of firing until 1,112°F (600°C). It's important to allow moisture to escape within the first firing and for other chemical compounds within the glaze to escape for the second firing.

Bisque firing schedule example:

Ramp 1: 212°F (100°C) p/h to 1,112°F (600°C)
Ramp 2: 302°F (150°C) p/h to 1,832°F (1,000°C)
Soak: Twenty minutes

Temperature ramps should relate to the thickness and size of your pieces. If you have made large pieces or have thick walls, you may need a slower-rising temperature to make sure the clay fires evenly throughout.

Packing a kiln for bisque fire

Loading a kiln for bisque firing is very similar to Tetris. You have the freedom of stacking pieces on top of one another or placing them side by side, with little or no space between them. After a little practice you will soon learn how certain items can be stacked and placed inside one another when production work is increased. Be very careful with stacking large amounts of work on top of one another, since bone-dry clay is very fragile and can easily break if handled and stacked incorrectly.

Try not to stack a heavy piece inside a delicate, light piece, since this will not withstand the weight and could potentially crack during firing. Everything needs to be supported well.

GLAZE FIRE

Glaze firings are usually the second firing, which happens after bisque firing.

Important steps before firing

- Use the same triangle prop technique as the bisque firing when placing the kiln shelves and props in your kiln.

- Do not stack work on top of one another when glaze firing. Pots should be *at least* 0.4 in. (1 cm) apart, since they will shrink and move around during the firing process. If your glazed pieces are too close or even touching, this can result in them fusing together.

- Wash your hands each time you handle a piece with a different glaze, since some oxides are very strong and can be transported onto another piece without you noticing.

- Try to glaze your pieces the day before you turn the kiln on. This will give the glazes enough time to fully dry out.

- During the glaze fire, some oxides can react with others if they are too close. Be aware of where you are placing certain items in your kiln. For example, a glaze that has chrome oxide or rutile in it will react with a tin white glaze.

Pieces glazed before glaze firing

The same pieces after glaze firing

Bat wash

To protect your kiln shelves from glaze accidents, apply a coating of bat wash. This is a white substance made from an alumina and silica mix. If a glaze you have used has run down your pot and onto the kiln shelf, it will be a lot easier to remove if you have bat wash on, since it acts as a barrier coating between the shelf and your pot. You can easily buy bat wash from a range of pottery suppliers. Mix the substance with water and brush/paint onto your shelves. Let this mixture dry before you place your pieces on it. Over time, the bat wash may start to flake, but you can easily reapply some more.

I have always been fascinated by how glaze colors change from before to after a firing. As you can see in the images on the left, powdery pastel shades turn to strong shiny and matte blues, greens, pinks, and whites.

How long does a glaze firing take?

On average a typical stoneware glaze firing may take up to eight or nine hours—depending on your kiln size and the amount of work you have inside—to reach temperature, plus another twenty-four hours to cool down before opening the kiln. This is why patience is so important in pottery. Cooling down too rapidly may cause problems for your pieces. Wait until the kiln temperature has reached at least 158°F (70°C) before you open the kiln. You could potentially harm your pieces if you open above this temperature—the extreme heat difference from a hot kiln to outside air flowing in may result in thermal shock and crazing.

Stoneware glaze-firing schedule example:

Ramp 1:   302°F (150°C) p/h to 1,112°F (600°C)
Ramp 2:   392°F (200°C) p/h to 2,264°F (1,240°C)
Soak: Twenty minutes

TAKING YOUR
PASSION TO THE
NEXT LEVEL

TAKING YOUR PASSION TO THE NEXT LEVEL
SETTING UP A STUDIO

You may be wondering how you can extend your pottery passion further after attending classes, to sharing a studio, becoming a member in a cooperative, setting up your own space, or even developing your skills with the intention to sell. I spent many years after university in my bedroom and living room making anything I could on a small desk without distracting my sister too much—this was mainly jewelry and small tile work. Of course, this couldn't last long; it's not a good idea living, working, and sleeping in the same room, let alone sharing that space with someone else.

It is such a great experience to share and work around other creative like-minded people when first starting out. I learned so much within the four years I shared a studio space at Roland Austin's pottery studio. I came straight from a ceramics course at university, so I was used to sharing large worktops, kilns, and materials, but Roland's space was a lot smaller, so this really helped me keep organized.

Below: My first working studio

Above: My studio now

There are many community studios around the world that have membership access in which you have full use of equipment, clay, and glazes. You may need to take lessons in that particular studio first to get a place, but these spaces are filled with creativity. It's a great place to start your journey with clay.

In 2016, I felt I was ready to progress my business further since I was receiving more commissions and getting many requests to start teaching. With my own space, I would be able to fulfill this.

My first proper studio was a blank canvas to set up my own way of working—as opposed to sharing with other students. A lot of work was needed to make the space work, since it was very small. I filled every wall as much as I could with shelves to hold my work, from freshly thrown to fired and glazed.

After a few years in my tiny studio, a larger space became available next door. Luckily it was sectioned off with a chipboard wall, which came down, and my smaller space opened up into a bigger workshop. I felt the only way for my business to grow was to get more space so I could teach more workshops and fulfill commissions. For me, teaching has always been an important side of my business.

Luckily, I have an outdoor space as well, which I can occasionally use with the very few months of sunshine we get in London.

There may be many obstacles and trial and error along the way when setting up your own studio, but try to see these stages as part of your progression. Obstacles are strongly linked to the way you set up your studio space. Make sure the layout of your studio equipment links in with your way of working. This can vary if you are hand-building and not using a pottery wheel.

Here is a list of points to consider for a clean, organized studio. Begin by always having a notepad or sketchbook nearby to document any ideas, notes, and glaze recipes.

Clay and working: Clay storage should be near your wheels or where you are working, so you don't have to carry heavy bags too far.

Try not to have freshly thrown work near your kiln when it's firing, since you don't want it to dry out too much before you start to trim it.

Electricity: You will need a reliable supply of electricity to run your kiln. Most other pottery equipment can be plugged into a standard socket. Check your kiln's usage. Is it three phase? If so, make sure this can be integrated into your space.

Flooring: Easy-to-clean floor (to use a mop and sponge) with no holes or dents, to avoid dust building up in those areas.

Glazes: Glaze buckets can be really heavy; make sure these are easily accessible. Ideally they sit on a platform with wheels.

Kiln: Your kiln needs to have a good amount of space around it for the heat to flow well. Make sure there is space around your kiln to store kiln shelves and kiln props.

Lighting: Natural light is good, but if this is not possible, then make sure you have good, bright lighting.

Location: Preferably a ground-level space, since ceramic equipment can be heavy, but if a lift is accessible, then even better.

Packing station: If you are selling your work online, in open studios, or even by commission, having packing materials readily available will keep you organized. These, if possible, should be away from your workstation and protected so they stay clean.

Plaster boards are best placed near your reclaim area, so you can easily transport the clay.

Raw ingredients should be well labeled in airtight containers and kept away from your clay.

Reclaim area
Reclaim buckets should be near to where you work with clay.

Ventilation: Make sure there are windows for ventilation to allow sufficient air flow.

Wall space: Wall space is extremely useful for attaching shelves, which will really help to store work, from greenware to trimmed, bone dry, glazed, and fired. If you have the space, these stages in making should have their own separate shelves. Storage space is a perennial problem. If you do not have sufficient wall space but have a wall or area, you can source a freestanding shelving unit; this will be really helpful.

Water: Water supply should be easily accessible, and a clay trap under your sink is a good idea.

You do not need a big budget to set up your own space. The most expensive piece of equipment is your wheel and kiln, which can even be bought secondhand. If you do not have a kiln, then there are many kiln-firing services in community studios that will allow you to bring your work and pay for it to be fired.

HEALTH AND SAFETY

Although pottery may not seem like a health hazard, there are many materials in a studio that can contribute to making a space unsafe to work in. Clay dust can be present without being obvious, and years of exposure can even result in silicosis from inhaling silica dust.

Regularly clean your surfaces with a wet sponge, including your workbench, since dust and other particles can settle and build up easily.

Mop your floor at least once a week.

Make sure your electricity supply is sufficient for your kiln and all other electrical equipment you will be using. Please read all instructions in the manual when purchasing your kiln.

Respiratory masks must be worn when mixing glazes or dealing with plaster and other dry ingredients.

Occasionally spray the air with water to allow dust to settle before mopping the floor.

Regularly wash your apron and all the clothes you wear in the studio. This should be done in your studio sink if you have a clay trap, since clay particles from your clothing and apron may build up in your washing machine.

An extraction fan can be attached to your kiln and directed out of a window to stop fumes and gases from being present in your studio.

MARKETING

Online

Having your own website is extremely beneficial for your business. It's a platform for you to showcase your work widely and for your audience to get to know you a little more.

Initially, I sold my work through various online marketplaces. This felt like a good starting point, a chance to really get stuck into learning about photography, product descriptions, and pricing. It can be very rewarding for customers to believe in your work from a small photo they see online. But ceramics is such a tactile material that it can be difficult for customers to visualize the true essence of textures, shapes, and colors.

Photography

I decided to invest in getting a photographer and stylist to capture my work, and it really changed my perspective. Some people are lucky enough to have the skills to do this all single-handedly, but after seeing images from the very first stylized shoot I had, I was amazed by how much better my work looked through the lens. After putting the photos up on my website, I realized how important photography and styling are. It sparked a new interest from a range of customers such as restaurant owners, coffee stores, and florists.

Fairs

Apart from an online presence, taking part in trade shows, on market stalls, at galleries, and at events is a great way to be seen—having customer interaction and hearing feedback is so important. I applied to as many fairs as I could when I started pottery. The preparation before the event, the setup, and the takedown can be tiring at times, but it can lead to something very special and might spark interest from new customers and businesses.

In 2017, I took part in a ceramics fair called the "Independent Ceramics Market" in Dalston, East London. I set up a small table with a few mugs, plates, and vases and was approached by a customer (James Hennebry) wanting to know prices for their new, soon-to-be-opening coffee store, called Rosslyn. A few meetings and phone calls later, I was supplying tumblers for Rosslyn to be used in their coffee shop, retail shelves, and online. Rosslyn's ethos, service, attention to detail, and uncompromising high quality have been credited throughout the world, and they were finalists in 2018's Best New Café in the World in the Sprudge Awards. Little did I know that Rosslyn's team would be so supportive of my business and really believe in my work. This great connection and commission has provided me with so much growth within my business.

WHY MISTAKES MATTER

This is a fundamental phrase I use constantly throughout my work. It can be frustrating waiting many hours to finally open the kiln from a firing, only to find out that your glaze hasn't worked, your plates have cracked, and the one pot you thought would come out spectacularly has been ruined by a mystery force in the kiln. All of these accidents will in the future be beneficial for you and your business. I keep a notepad handy in my studio to write down any notes about the pieces I make. Just in case something goes wrong in the kiln, I can possibly rectify these by looking over my notes.

I have learned throughout sixteen years of working with clay that there are so many aspects to learn, whether it's at the very beginning of knowing what clay to use, or at the very end with understanding glazing. Mistakes make you grow further; without all the mistakes I have made throughout my time working with clay, I wouldn't be where I am today.

You don't need to know every little detail before you start your business; otherwise you will begin to overthink. Most of what we make the first time around consists of trial and error, and we shouldn't be afraid of this. Your ideas will change and evolve over time.

Experiment, make mistakes, develop, and learn!

Photos from Rosslyn Coffee store,
78 Queen Victoria Street, London EC4N 4SJ

155

GLOSSARY

GLOSSARY

alumina Glaze stiffener used as a raw ingredient in glaze making

bat wash White powder consisting of alumina and silica. Once mixed with water, it can be applied to kiln shelves to protect them from glaze damage.

bisque (bisquit) First firing, turning unfired clay into ready-to-glaze ceramic

calcium borate frit Used as a flux and glass former in glazes. Higher quantities are used in earthenware glazes.

chamfered An angled edge, found mainly on the bases of pots to elevate them from the surface they are sitting on

chattering A rippled texture often found in the trimming stages. Caused by blunt tools or not holding the turning tool firmly.

china clay Used as a stiffening agent in glaze recipes

coning (throwing) A method of clay preparation to reduce air pockets before making a pot on the wheel

crawling A glaze fault caused by overfiring, or an error within the glaze mixture

crazing A glaze fault caused by tension between the glaze and clay body

crosshatch(ing) A technique used to score the clay's surface before attaching another piece to it. It can be used for handles and many hand-building techniques.

diamond pad Abrasive pad used to sand work after firing

dolomite Calcium magnesium carbonate. Depending on quantities used, it can produce a matte finish.

earthenware Low-temperature pottery-firing range

fettle To neaten up faults in glaze decoration or greenware, using a knife

frit A combination of glaze ingredients, when melted together are rendered insoluble, making any toxic material safe to use

flux An ingredient in a glaze and clay that reacts with silica in order for it to melt and form a glaze or glass

foot ring A feature at the base of a pot

greenware Unfired clay in its raw state

glaze A powdery and liquid substance, once prepared, applied, and fired, turns to a thin layer of glass that coats a pot

grog A.k.a. grit. Ceramic that is ground and fired, then applied to clay to enhance stability and provide a textured surface.

homogenized Particles of clay combined together

kidney A.k.a. "rib." Rubber, metal, or wooden tool shaped like a kidney and used to smooth out interior and exterior walls, and to generally shape clay in many ways

kiln Equipment used to fire clay and turn it into ceramic

kiln wash A.k.a. bat wash, used to protect kiln furniture

leather-hard A hardening stage in a clay's journey when it can be handled, trimmed, and carved without distorting too much

matte A nonshiny glaze surface

oxide Natural metal elements that are ground to a powder and can be used as a colorant in a glaze recipe

plaster A fine white powder made from calcium sulfate hemihydrate. When mixed with the correct amount of water, it is left to dry and harden. Widely used in pottery studios for molds, wedging, and slip casting.

plaster bat Block of plaster used to reclaim and wedge clay on

porcelain A white clay body; when fired to a high temperature, a translucent quality is formed.

porous A surface that holds in moisture

potash feldspar Used as a flux in a glaze. Depending on the quantities used, it will produce a shiny surface in a glaze.

potter's needle Thin metal pointed tool used to release air pockets, to cut into clay, and to test the thickness of the base of a pot

potter's wire Thin metal wire to cut through clay and to take pieces off the pottery wheel

pulling A method used to obtain height in a wall when working on the wheel. It is also used in conjunction with handle making.

pyrometric cones Small devices placed inside a kiln to gauge heat work during a firing

pyrometer An instrument connected to a thermocouple that is fixed inside a kiln to detect the temperature during the firing process

quartz A mineral often known as silica powder, used in glazes

raw glazing Glazing a greenware pot before bisque firing

reclaim Method used to prolong the life of unfired clay.

rim The top surface of a pot

serrated kidney A jagged-edge rubber/silicone kidney used to make textured work

silica A glass-forming ingredient found in clay and glaze. Used in conjunction with a flux to aid melting during firing.

slip Clay mixed with water to produce a liquid clay. Slip can be used to join handles to pots in greenware stages and for casting in molds.

slurry A mushy liquid often produced when mixing clay with water from making work on the wheel. It can be mixed with clay trimmings for reclaiming purposes.

soaking When a kiln has reached its desired temperature, a soak allows the whole kiln to heat up to this temperature and remain there for a short amount of time.

stain Manufactured powder or liquid form used as a colorant in glazes

stoneware A high-fired temperature range, and clay that becomes vitrified at temperatures above 2,192°F (1,200°C)

tin oxide An opacifier and colorant added to a clear glaze to produce a white finish

thermocouple A probe inserted inside a kiln connected to a digital kiln controller to detect the temperature during firing

throwing A method in pottery to produce three-dimensional forms. Clay is placed on a wheel that rotates clockwise/counterclockwise in order to produce a variety of shapes.

turning/trimming A method in pottery to shape and refine a piece that has already been thrown or hand built. Sharp metal turning tools are used in this process.

vitrification When chemical compounds react in extreme heat, resulting in a nonporous material

wax resist/emulsion A liquid substance applied to bisqueware to resist glaze application

wedging Clay preparation to remove air pockets and to fully combine clay platelets

wheel head The main part of the potter's wheel, made from metal and used to shape and form pottery pieces

whiting Calcium carbonate. Used in glaze recipes to strengthen the glaze.

wooden bat A circular wooden board placed on top of a wheel to throw pots on. It can also be used for hand-building purposes.

www.melisadora.com

DEDICATION

I would like to dedicate this book to Leo (my nephew) and Mina (my niece), who I hope will one day enjoy working with clay as much as I do.

ACKNOWLEDGMENTS

Thank you to my parents, Lydia and Korehan, and my sister, Yasemin, for their continuous support and guidance from the very beginning. To all my friends for your encouragement and putting up with me talking about this book nonstop for the past year, especially Kate, Becks, Steph, Steffi, and Holly. Thank you to my partner, Joao, who throughout this process has provided me with so much enthusiasm, inspirational ideas, and positivity.

To Roland Austin for his generosity of knowledge in pottery and for making my four years in his studio so memorable and special.

Thank you to those I have worked with over the years, all my tutors at university, and my students. Your support and guidance has enabled me to inspire others with writing this book.

Art director: Aurélien Farjon

Photographer: Alexander Edwards, all photographs except

Contents page: Lucy Richards
Pages 150, 160: Leanne Dixon
Page 154: Floristry, Kasia Borowiecka